From Property to Partner:

Women's Progress and Political Resistance

Sheila Suess Kennedy

&

Morton J. Marcus

Book design by Niina Cochran
Cover art by Elizabeth Mahoney, EM Design
Publication production by Anne Laker, Laker Verbal LLC

Table of Contents

Introduction

In 1964, Bob Dylan wrote a song that became an anthem for the turbulent 60s. Its lyrics are no less applicable today. The first stanza warns listeners that they live in a time of unsettling social change, and the second admits that the direction of change is always uncertain—"the wheel's still in spin, and there's no tellin' who that it's namin'."

Come gather 'round people
Wherever you roam
And admit that the waters
Around you have grown
And accept it that soon
You'll be drenched to the bone
If your time to you is worth savin'
And you better start swimmin'
Or you'll sink like a stone
For the times they are a-changin'

Come writers and critics
Who prophesize with your pen
And keep your eyes wide
The chance won't come again
And don't speak too soon
For the wheel's still in spin
And there's no tellin' who
That it's namin'
For the loser now
Will be later to win
For the times they are a-changin'

The United States is—not for the first time—experiencing a period of rapid and disorienting social change. A variety of authoritarian, racist, and sexist groups are reacting by mounting ferocious assaults on democratic norms and the rule of law. Christian Nationalists currently control the Republican Party and have turned that once-respectable center-right party into a far-right appendage of a disgraced former President who still commands the fidelity of most of its members. The Supreme Court is dominated by a reactionary Christianist majority, and Congress is

1

gridlocked by gerrymandering and the operation of outmoded electoral and legislative processes, including but not limited to the filibuster.

America is very clearly at a critical juncture. It is not an exaggeration to say that a Republican sweep in November of 2022 would have made it incredibly difficult to resist the tide of reaction, and would have threatened the very continuation of democratic governance by We the People.

The 2022 Midterm elections thus provided a critical test: would the usual history of such contests—significant losses by the party in power—prevail, plunging the nation further into uncharted and treacherous waters? Or would those midterms prove to be a pivot point, a rejection of those attempting to turn the wheel backward, the occasion for an angry electorate to say "enough"? And if the electorate finally *did* say "enough," to what could we attribute that welcome (but arguably delayed) awakening?

We think the answer is women.

Chapter One: An Overview

Sheila Kennedy

This is a pivotal moment for America but also for women's rights. Defenders of patriarchy are arguing for traditional familial roles. The U.S. Supreme Court is dominated by justices who are overprotective of claims that legal protection of female autonomy violates religious freedom and underprotective of federal authority to make state governments respect women's basic civil liberties. A once respectable center-right political party has embraced a radical Christian Nationalism characterized in part by retrograde beliefs about "women's place." Given those realities, it is time to take stock—to analyze the "staying power" of the various technological and social changes that have facilitated women's movement into the mainstream of American life and to assess the power and prospects of those organizations and individuals who are intent upon reversing that progress.

What comes next is not yet another argument for women's rights; we begin with the conviction that those rights are an important social good. Instead, we are exploring the social, economic, and technological innovations that facilitated the movement of large numbers of women into the workforce and political life and the social, political, and economic implications of that movement. We will examine both the under-appreciated historical connections that have forced, facilitated, or retarded acceptance of women's rights and the ways in which women's progress is (or is not) reordering the culture. We especially want to consider the roots, extent, and probable consequences of the current backlash, including but not limited to the fierce resistance to female reproductive autonomy and abortion.

Due to the breadth of our inquiry, which touches on everything from economics, science and technology, politics, political philosophy, and religion, we have interviewed experts in several fields to augment our own research. That said, this is not intended to be an academic treatise; our goal is to translate scholarly research into readable and accessible information for a wider audience and to illuminate the roots of the very real "battle of the sexes" that is currently threatening women's progress—and thus, we would argue, America's.

Over the past two hundred years, several of America's most profound social changes have been a consequence of growing autonomy in the status of women. The drive to expand female rights began slowly and then accelerated; while it took a century for the U.S. suffragette movement to secure the vote for women, access to education and employment improved somewhat more rapidly. Along the way, women's progress has engendered considerable resistance and blowback, primarily because cultural attitudes generally are slow to change, but also because social change is rarely welcomed by those occupying superior or privileged social positions.

We are experiencing a blowback now, as a number of state legislatures rush to take advantage of a recent Supreme Court decision reversing—for the first time in American legal history—a previously settled constitutional right. The Court has ruled that females do not have constitutionally protected bodily autonomy—that is, that women do not have the right to make their own reproductive decisions—opening the way for a number of highly gerrymandered red states to enact drastic restrictions on a woman's ability to make her own decisions about whether and/or when she will have children.

Until the Supreme Court decision in *Dobbs v. Jackson Women's Health Organization* (hereafter *Dobbs*), conventional wisdom had held that most of the progress women have achieved is now firmly embedded in America's social fabric; it has become commonplace to see women as CEOs, news anchors, soccer stars, and political leaders. Nevertheless, despite the significant changes in majority attitudes that have accompanied women's progress, Americans are encountering concerted efforts to roll back many of those advances and limit women's right to self-determination. Recently, with the ascendency of five ideologically right-wing justices to the U. S. Supreme Court, those efforts have been given increased momentum, raising fundamental questions about American law, the clash of some people's religious beliefs with civil liberties, and the ultimate outcome of this fierce debate over the status of half the country's population.

At its core, at least in the United States, the women's movement has been an effort to achieve the personal, moral, and political autonomy promised by the Bill of Rights. A fair reading of that document and its history discloses an underlying commitment to what has been called the libertarian principle: citizens—including female citizens—have the right to direct their own lives and pursue their own life goals free of government interference until and unless they harm the person or property of another, and so long as they are willing to grant an equal liberty to others.

This American belief in the right of each individual to self-determination grew out of the Enlightenment's focus on human rights and the works of philosophers who preceded the Founders. In 1859, that right to self-determination was stated definitively by John Stuart Mill. In *On Liberty*, Mill defended the right of individuals to pursue their own personal goals: "The only part of the conduct of anyone for which he is amenable to society is that which concerns others. In the part which merely concerns himself, his independence is, of right, absolute. Over himself, over his own body and mind, the individual is sovereign." (If written today, some would object to Mill's choice of pronouns.)

What constitutes a harm justifying government intervention remains a matter of considerable debate, and the notion that this sovereign right of self-ownership applies to women and people of color as well as to White men is relatively recent—and its acceptance, as we are learning, remains hard-fought.

As women have struggled to surmount the cultural, legal, and political barriers they have faced, both men and women have either come to terms with or resisted the consequential changes to longstanding domestic and economic arrangements. The transition of roughly half the population from the status of property to a position of equal citizenship has transformed the nation in unforeseen ways, and it has been experienced as profoundly destabilizing by many Americans, especially the White Christian men who continue to exercise disproportionate social authority in the United States.

This book attempts to "connect the dots" between the ongoing struggles for women's progress and the social, economic, and political environment we currently inhabit. Will women retain their hard-won rights over the frenzied resistance to female emancipation? Will women find it necessary to continue the long struggle to have their rights reaffirmed? Will the current backlash subside, allowing American citizens of all genders, colors, and orientations to achieve equal protection under the law and a measure of domestic tranquility?

Hazarding answers to those questions requires a "deep dive" into the social, legal, economic, and technological innovations that have facilitated the movement of large numbers of women into the workforce and into civic and political life. What are the social, political, and economic implications of that progress? How is women's emancipation reordering the culture and America's political landscape? What are the roots of the fierce and sustained resistance to women's equality, and what do the wellsprings of that resistance tell us about the future?

Examining these and related questions is the key to understanding the historical connections that have forced, facilitated, or retarded women's progress. Our approach to that task rests on the perspectives we bring to the inquiry, so it seems appropriate to make explicit both our preconceptions and the nature of the questions we will explore.

Who are we? The authors of this book are longtime friends, academics with significant life experience beyond the classroom. We agree about certain things and disagree about others. One of us is male, one female, and we are both products of the 20th century. We have different backgrounds and preoccupations and rather different communication styles, as you will see in our individually authored chapters, but we are in agreement on the broad outlines of policies advancing the status of American women.

Sheila Suess Kennedy is Emerita Professor of Law and Public Policy at the O'Neill School of Public and Environmental Affairs at Indiana University. Until her retirement, she was a faculty fellow with both the Center for Religion and American Culture and the Tobias Center for Leadership Excellence, an adjunct professor of political science, and founder of the University's Center for Civic Literacy. Prior to joining the faculty in 1998, she practiced law in Indianapolis, including a stint as Corporation Counsel for the City from 1977 to 1980, when she left to become the Republican candidate for Indiana's then 11th Congressional District seat. From 1992 to 1998 she was Executive Director of the Indiana ACLU. She is the author of nine books and numerous academic articles and publishes a daily blog devoted to politics and public policy.

Morton J. Marcus taught economics at Indiana University's Kelley School of Business and served as Director of the Indiana Business Research Center. His work focused on the demographic and economic changes in the Indiana economy. He relates these dynamics, in their national and international perspectives, to citizens, businesses, and governments throughout the state and nation via articles, public presentations, TV and radio programs, plus a weekly newspaper column and podcast.

The two of us share the following convictions that shape our perspectives on the history we will be exploring:

> • We believe that precision in language matters. Readers deserve to know how we are defining the terms that we use. We begin with the shared conviction that the term **women's movement** encompasses two different elements: **women's liberation**, on the one hand, and that portion of the **feminist movement** that advocates for **parity**, on the other. Liberation is the process of eliminating legal and social barriers to equality; parity is insistence on equal representation in various institutions

of American life, like legislatures, corporate boards, and other organizations that wield authority. (Still to be considered is the concept of **equity**, a sense of fairness, a moral judgment.) We have seen the demand for parity manifested in the recently struck-down California law that required companies to elect a certain number of women to their corporate boards. [1]

• We believe a fair reading of history confirms that sustained social change comes through incremental evolution, not revolution. Activists who demand that social attitudes and behaviors change immediately to meet their most recent, exacting expectations are being both unrealistic and unfair. A personal anecdote may illustrate what we mean: Sheila Kennedy attended law school in the early 1970s and interviewed for positions at local law firms at a time when women lawyers were rare. As she tells it, "Serial interviews with prospective associates were conducted by several of the partners, and I was in conversation with two who were being very careful not to ask improper questions—this was barely ten years after creation of the EEOC.[2] Since I had three children, I thought it reasonable to volunteer my childcare arrangements. One of the partners was so obviously relieved that I didn't seem to be some sort of radical feminist, he blurted out, 'It isn't that there's anything wrong with being a woman. We hired a man with a glass eye once!'"

"It would be easy to dismiss a man who equated female gender with disability—to categorize him as an irredeemably sexist example of a bygone era. But the firm hired me, and four or five years later, when I ran for Congress, that partner enthusiastically supported my campaign and held a fundraiser for me. Like all of us, he was a product of his time, and his initial reactions were consistent with the culture he'd grown up in. As that

---

[1] We like the response by late Supreme Court Justice Ruth Bader Ginsberg to the question "How many women should be on the Supreme Court?" Ginsberg replies that there will be "enough" women on the Court when there are nine. As she clearly recognized, quotas can easily become floors.

[2] The Equal Employment Opportunities Commission.

culture changed, so did he. Some people don't change; many others do."

• Both of us believe in cutting folks a bit of slack. We agree that identity is more complicated and ambiguous than many people want to believe. Men are not from Mars and women are not from Venus. Although there are significant biological differences that deserve recognition and accommodation, we believe that it is the differential socialization from birth that has denied both genders, not to mention gender-fluid folks, freedom of self-identification.

This rigid approach to socialization can lead to essentialism, the belief that all members of an observably different group share certain attributes that are "essential" elements of their identity, and essentialism is an element of bigotry. Essentialism fosters beliefs that all Blacks are lazy, all Asians are good at math and science, all gay men are "sissies," all Jews are sharp business people, or all Whites are racists. Similarly, the widespread assumptions that all women are nurturing and that all men are aggressive and interested only in making sexual conquests are essentialist beliefs that infect otherwise beneficial efforts to level the playing field.

A recent example comes from the #MeToo movement. When #MeToo emerged, we both applauded. Morton Marcus had witnessed and Kennedy had encountered unwanted approaches from men ranging from boorish behaviors to significantly worse, and we both recognized the unfairness of blaming the victim, where complaints about sexual assaults were dismissed with "well, what was she wearing?" or other responses suggesting that the woman was somehow "asking for it." Holding predators, not their victims, responsible was long overdue. Sending a message that unwanted touching and worse are not amusing, not a male prerogative, and not to be tolerated was also long overdue. That said, there is a difference between unwanted attention and assault. Inappropriate behaviors occur on a continuum; responses should be calibrated to the severity of the behavior. Furthermore, fundamental fairness requires rejecting essentialism—all men are not dogs, and all women are not saints. Taking women seriously is not the same thing as uncritically believing anything and everything any woman says. An accusation of impropriety or assault should be considered a rebuttable presumption, where it is true until and unless there is probative evidence to the contrary.

• Both of us also believe that women's legal, political, and economic equality isn't just a good thing, it is critically important. Our contemporary society faces massive social and ecological problems; we will need the talents and intellect of every part of our population to address those problems. As we trace the decline of women's subservience and second-class citizenship, we see a trajectory that advances everyone's prospects and wellbeing. Of all of the perspectives we bring to this account, our firm belief in the importance of women's continued progress is paramount.

• Further, we both believe that American policymakers are overdue in acknowledging the contributions made by women and men who provide uncompensated care for others, including but not limited to the multiple domestic tasks that make it possible for others in the household to engage in paid employment.

• Finally, we both believe in the importance of *evidence*, and in the elements that constitute credible evidence. As the old academic saying has it, "Anecdotes are not data." Anecdotes may be usefully employed to illustrate an issue (see above!), but conclusions about the social or political effects of any particular event or series of events require field-tested research, preferably peer-reviewed, or its equivalent. Your uncle's rant at Thanksgiving may or may not reflect widespread public opinion.

With the preliminaries out of the way, let's begin.

Chapter Two: Patriarchy and the Culture War

Sheila Kennedy

Let's begin with the obvious: there are genuine biological differences between men and women, and those differences profoundly and understandably shaped human cultures for thousands of years. Over time, science and technology have operated to minimize the social impact of those differences, although the differences themselves remain. In addition to changes in the job market that have made physical strength less important and inventions that significantly reduced the time spent on housework, women can now plan, defer or abstain from procreation without the necessity of celibacy, a reality that allows them to pursue educational and career choices that used to be available exclusively to men. Those choices have facilitated their ability to participate more fully in civic and political life.

Despite those advances, the drive for gender equity in the workplace and polity continues to be hindered by the persistence of attitudes and traditions more appropriate to bygone generations, and especially by religious beliefs that powerfully influence the country's politics and culture. As the second section of this chapter will explain, a number of religious denominations work assiduously to impose their doctrinal beliefs about women (and what they believe to be their proper, subordinate place in society) through legislation applicable to everyone. Those theological positions support and strengthen a cultural patriarchy rooted in history, politics, and privilege. As we will see, religious arguments are used to justify the still-significant resistance to women's personal autonomy and to motivate the increasingly frantic efforts of the political Right to reverse women's social, legal, and economic progress.

Biology and Destiny

For generations, there have been two major biological impediments to women's equal participation in society and especially in the workforce: women's relative lack of physical strength vis-a-vis their male counterparts and the fact that women get pregnant. Those two realities have exerted a major effect on cultural attitudes about men and women. For a very long time, most jobs required manual labor—and often brute strength—and most (although not all) females were physically unable to undertake such tasks. Over the years, as technology has improved, the job market has also changed and fewer jobs today require physical strength. An increasing number instead require education, intellect, and/or particular skills, qualifications that are more evenly distributed between the genders and even, in some cases, are more likely to be possessed by women.

In 2020, Janet Yellen authored a report for the Brookings Institution that focused on the 20th-century history of women's employment. Early in the century, she noted, most women in the United States didn't work outside the home, and the few who did were primarily young and unmarried. A mere 20 percent of all women were "gainful workers," and only 5 percent of those were married. Yellen did point out that those statistics understated the economic contributions of married women who worked from home in family businesses and/or in the home production of goods for sale. The statistics also obscured racial difference: African-American women were about twice as likely to participate in the labor force as White women at the time, and were more likely to remain in the labor force after marriage. When women did work outside the home, it was often taken as evidence that the husband was unwilling or unable to support the household. As a result, men tended to view a wife's paid employment as a shameful statement on the husband's role as a breadwinner. As Yellen wrote,

> "The fact that many women left work upon marriage reflected cultural norms, the nature of the work available to them, and legal strictures. The occupational choices of those young women who did work were severely circumscribed. Most women lacked significant education, and women with little education mostly toiled as piece workers in factories or as domestic workers, jobs that were dirty and often unsafe. Educated women were scarce. Fewer than 2 percent of all 18- to 24-year-olds were enrolled in an institution of higher education, and just one-third of those were women. Such women did not have to perform manual labor, but their choices were likewise constrained."

As Yellen notes and many of us vividly remember, there was widespread sentiment against women, especially married women, working outside the home. Even in the face of severely limited opportunities, however, increasing numbers of women did continue to enter the labor force during this period. As a result, some 50 percent of single women worked by 1930 as did nearly 12 percent of married women. Mores and social attitudes were slowly changing, partly as a result of what is often referred to as the "first wave" of the women's movement, which focused on suffrage and (to a lesser extent) temperance, and which culminated in the ratification of the 19th Amendment in 1920, giving all American women the right to vote.

Between the 1930s and mid-1970s, women's participation in the economy, especially the participation of married women, continued to rise, spurred by several social changes. The growth of mass high school education was accompanied by a similar rise in graduation rates. New technologies led to an increased demand for clerical workers, and clerical jobs were seen as appropriate for women because they tended to be cleaner and safer. And while there were still bizarre rules that kept many women out of the labor force—for example, female librarians in most cities could not be married, and female school teachers who became pregnant were dismissed once they "showed"—these restrictions gradually disappeared following World War II.[3]

By far the most consequential change, the development that eliminated the major impediment to women's full participation in economic and civic life, was the introduction of reliable contraception, primarily although not exclusively, the birth control pill.

Before the advent of reliable birth control, every sexual encounter carried the risk of pregnancy, and pregnancy generally meant the end of a woman's economic independence. A pregnant woman was almost always unemployable; for that matter, a married woman in her childbearing years was similarly unemployable, since there was always the possibility of pregnancy and the resulting need to care for offspring, seen as a uniquely female responsibility. Most women were therefore economically dependent upon the men to whom they were married. (Refusing to marry was no panacea: unmarried women were routinely labeled "old maids," and were objects of pity and/or derision.) If her marriage was unhappy or worse, violent, a woman with children was literally enslaved; given the barriers she faced to participation in the workforce and her resulting inability to support herself and her offspring, she usually couldn't leave. Absent charitable intervention or inherited wealth, or friends or relatives willing to house and feed her and her children, she was totally dependent on her husband's earnings.

Access to reliable contraception—and in situations where that contraception failed, abortion—was thus absolutely essential to women's independence. If women could plan when to procreate, they could also plan when not to procreate. They could choose to schedule or defer motherhood in order to pursue education and career opportunities. The availability of the birth control pill didn't simply liberate millions of

---

[3] However, it wasn't until 1986 that United Airlines was ordered to pay $33 million in back pay and to reinstate 475 flight attendants who had been forced to quit in the mid-1960s because of a no-marriage rule.

women, opening possibilities that had been foreclosed by reasons of biology, its availability and widespread use triggered enormous changes in social attitudes that in turn opened the door to legislation that advanced both women's economic independence and their ability to more fully participate in the civic life of the nation.

A 2010 article in *Forbes* marking the fiftieth anniversary of the birth control pill acknowledged its immense significance. The article began by noting the then-current workforce status of women:

> "For the first time in U.S. history, women have overtaken men in the workplace. More specifically, they've overtaken men in professional roles. As of 2009, women represented half of all U.S. workers and are the primary or co-breadwinners in nearly two-thirds of American households. That's a far cry from 1967, when women made up only one-third of all U.S. workers."

Without the birth control pill, women would almost certainly not have made it into powerful senior positions. While the political and social will to bring a critical mass of women into the workplace was certainly there through the advent of the birth control pill, which coincided with the second wave of feminism and the fight for equal rights, the pill gave women a tangible tool to level the playing field with men. They no longer had to be mothers first and careerists second. The pill allowed for both their entrance and ascendance in the workplace.

There's no denying that the pill triggered a sexual revolution for women as well. Because they no longer had to worry about getting pregnant, it freed them up to have sex outside of marriage. But it was the workplace where the pill made its most lasting impact.

Together with women's new prominence in political and economic life, that sexual revolution, such as it was (the punditry continues to argue about its nature, extent, and consequences), ran headlong into what is perhaps the most regressive element of American culture: fundamentalist religion.

The current assault on women's autonomy, led primarily by people espousing fundamentalist versions of Evangelical Christianity, has awakened many Americans to the considerable influence of religion on American law and culture. That influence is not new, although the extent of it has largely gone unrecognized. Indeed, through most of American history, people have vastly underestimated the profound and continuing influence of culturally embedded attitudes that originated with religious ways of interpreting reality. Most of us today recognize the impact of purportedly religious beliefs on issues like abortion, same-sex marriage, and support for the death penalty, but what is far less obvious is the degree to which religiously rooted worldviews continue to influence seemingly secular policy debates, including economic policies.

Many of the cultural perspectives that shape our policy preferences were originally religious, and those religious roots have influenced our adult worldviews—including the worldviews of people who reject theological doctrines and do not believe themselves to be religious. The religiously centered values debate isn't a conflict between people who are religious and people who are not, nor is it a struggle between people holding different religious beliefs. It's a debate between people operating out of different and largely inconsistent worldviews, and whether they recognize it or not, many of those worldviews originally grew out of different and frequently inconsistent religious explanations of the world we inhabit. Those inconsistencies don't just reflect differences between major religions, i.e., different theological approaches taken by Judaism, Christianity, Islam, etc., but also between denominations within those religions, especially the numerous denominations within Christianity. Calvinist beliefs, for example, continue to exert a major influence on American economic policy.

As women have slowly moved into the mainstream of American life, the doctrinal and structural differences of the major Abrahamic religions have shaped both their official responses and the culture. That has especially been true of religions like Catholicism that prohibit women from the priesthood and consider both abortion and artificial birth control sinful. It wasn't until 2020 that Pope Francis changed church law to allow a somewhat expanded role for women within the Catholic Church. The decree allows women to serve as readers, altar servers, and assistants to priests during service or in administering Holy Communion; however, the priesthood remains exclusively male.

> As Frank Bruni has written, "For all the remarkable service that the Catholic Church performs, it is one of the world's dominant and most unshakable patriarchies, with tenets that don't abet equality."

For women to get a fair shake in the workforce, they need at least some measure of reproductive freedom. But Catholic bishops in the United States lobbied strenuously against the Obamacare requirement that employers such as religiously affiliated schools and hospitals include coverage for contraception in workers' health insurance.

The autocratic structure of Catholicism, which discourages dissent from approved messaging and requires the exclusion of women from the pulpit, operates to reinforce the subordinate status of women. Recent revelations about an internal "faith group" within Catholicism underscore that message. People of Praise, which counts current Supreme Court Justice Amy Coney Barrett among its members and calls for complete obedience of women to their husbands, "emphasizes the importance of childbirth, pregnancy, and the abandonment of autonomy and privacy it supposedly entails, as a core part of what it means to be a woman."[4] The Catholic Church remains adamantly anti-abortion, recognizing an exception only when it is clearly required in order to save the life of the mother.

The response of liberal Protestantism to cultural change has been very different. The largest mainline Protestant denominations include the United Methodist Church (UMC), the Evangelical Lutheran Church in America (ELCA), the Presbyterian Church (PC-USA), the Episcopal Church, the American Baptist Church (ABC- USA, not to be confused with the Southern Baptists considered below), the United Church of Christ (UCC), and the Christian Church Disciples of Christ (DOC). Sometimes referred to as the "Seven Sisters," these denominations have seen significant growth in the ordination of women; as of 2010, approximately 10 percent of Protestant pastors were female. A survey conducted in 1987 suggested that women entering pastoral positions brought liberal commitments in religion, theological discussions, and cultural values to their congregations. Those commitments translate into their current supportive positions on abortion and birth control; a recent study by Pew categorizes them as supportive of abortion rights, albeit with some restrictions.

When it comes to religion and women's rights, historians note that Quakers and Jews have been long-standing and prominent proponents of female equality. Quakers are among the least "top down" of Christian sects, and as far back as the early 1800s, Quaker women who were recognized as being "called" were allowed to travel to share their gifts of ministry, usually with a chaperone. The most famous was probably Lucretia Mott (1793-1880), known for her activism in the anti-slavery and early women's rights movements. The Quaker acceptance of women's education and ministry set Quakers apart from the rest of organized Christianity and may explain the disproportionate presence of abolitionists among Quaker women. Anti-slavery work led to gatherings of women who were also concerned about the need for greater rights for women. Of the four women who led the planning for the first Women's Rights Convention in Seneca Falls in 1848, three were Quakers.

---

[4] "Revealed: leaked video shows Amy Coney Barrett's secretive faith group drove women to tears" by Stephanie Kirchgaessner, https://www.theguardian.com/us-news/2022/aug/26/amy-coney-barrett-faith-group-people-of-praise [accessed 9/4/22]

Like Quakerism, Judaism has no single authority able to prescribe what is "kosher" in Jewish law and observance. Throughout the ages, rabbis have argued about the proper meaning of biblical and Talmudic passages, and individual Jews have followed those that they found persuasive. Women's status has varied, but the prevailing attitudes have usually been more progressive than those in surrounding cultures. In Judaism, descent is matrilinear: a Jew is someone born of a Jewish mother. Jewish law requires women to obey the same negative commandments that men must follow (the "thou shalt nots") but excuses them from ritual duties that are time-bound, presumably in recognition of women's maternal obligations. As far back as Talmudic times, evidence suggests that at least some women were educated in the Bible and Jewish law. During and after the Middle Ages, because many Jewish women were the family breadwinners in order to allow the man of the house to study, the culture has been very accepting of women entering the workforce and later the professions. With respect to worship, progress has been more recent: Reform Judaism ordained its first female rabbi in 1972, and Reconstructionist Judaism followed suit in 1974. Today, there are more than a thousand women in the rabbinate as well as a growing number of LGBTQ rabbis, and congregants are accustomed to seeing women as rabbis and cantors within Reform, Conservative, and Reconstructionist synagogues.

The Orthodox movement within Judaism has been considerably slower to accept women's full participation; in Orthodox synagogues, men and women still sit apart, and until very recently there have been no female rabbis. Feminists within Orthodoxy have been actively advocating for reforms, and in 2013 the first group of female rabbinical students graduated from a New York seminary, but there is still considerable resistance within Orthodoxy to giving them pulpits and to many of the changes that the Reform, Reconstructionist, and Conservative movements have made.

With respect to abortion, Jewish law affirms that protecting existing life is paramount at all stages of pregnancy; however, Judaism does not consider a fetus a person until the head emerges from the womb. In Jewish law, the interests of the pregnant individual always come before that of the fetus. Jewish sources explicitly state that abortion is not only permitted but is required should the pregnancy endanger the life or health of the pregnant individual, and "health" includes psychological as well as physical health.

American Muslims have only recently been numerous enough to affect social attitudes about women in the U.S. Worldwide Islamic practices vary widely. The Koran does require the education of women and gives women certain rights if divorced by their husbands. According to the Institute for Social Policy and Understanding, U.S. Muslims are more likely than White

Evangelicals and Protestants to have favorable views of feminists. The Institute has found that "American Muslim women denounce gender discrimination inside and outside of their community."

Evangelicals and the Status of Women

Evangelicals, like the rest of America's religious landscape, are diverse; however, the more fundamentalist White Evangelical Christian denominations are currently united in their opposition to women's reproductive autonomy. That contemporary reality has tended to obscure the history of American Evangelicalism, which was far from monolithic in its approach to gender and considerably less political than today. In some Evangelical denominations, women were allowed to be ordained and otherwise vested with spiritual authority; in many others, women were—and still are—forbidden from holding leadership roles.

A major tenet of Evangelical Christianity is the doctrine of complementarianism—the belief that while men and women are equal in creation, they are distinct in function. Biblical womanhood reflects this belief in "separate spheres." Men are to be the leaders of the church and the home, and women are meant to support and submit to them. This doctrine has a long history in the Southern Baptist Convention (SBC), one of the largest and most influential of the Evangelical churches. As religious historians have reported, Southern Baptist leader John Broadus (1827-1895) answered the question "Should women speak in mixed public assemblies?" with a definitive "no" in 1889. The year before, when Southern Baptist women formed the Woman's Missionary Union, they assured male leaders that they only desired to be supportive, not independent as women in some other denominations were.

As one writer has noted, that thinking, advanced by the world's largest organization for Protestant women, "shaped the views of generations of Southern Baptist women and in turn those of their Evangelical neighbors and friends." This approach to the roles of men and women persisted; in 1974, the wife of one influential Southern Baptist pastor wrote to a widely approving audience that the man should lead and the woman should be submissive.

As the broader American culture changed, some Southern Baptist women pushed the denomination to rethink that submission. The SBC held a consultation on women's roles in 1978, and a later organization, Baptist Women in Ministry, argued for an expanded role for women within the denomination. Within the broader Evangelical movement, there were also challenges to complementarianism and the traditional understanding of women's roles. In 1988, Christians for Biblical Equality sought to empower women in Evangelical churches. About the same time, the Council on Biblical Manhood and Womanhood was formed to revisit the accepted definition of biblically appropriate gender roles.

These efforts largely failed. In 2000, despite the emergence of Evangelical women arguing for more equal status within the faith, the SBC reaffirmed its adherence to complementarianism, publishing a proclamation that wives should submit to their husbands and pastors should be male.

Evangelical theology doesn't simply elevate men over women; it considers homosexuality and gender-fluid identities to be sinful and unnatural and rejects efforts to secure equal legal rights for LGBTQ Americans. As Evangelicals have moved into the current political arena and as the Republican Party has become more and more dependent upon the Evangelical vote, those beliefs have powered what has come to be called the Culture War, essentially the transformation of Evangelical theology into a political movement. Any effort to examine Evangelical theology today must contend with the fact that, in today's America, Evangelical is not simply a religious descriptor; it has become a political label.

Numerous studies have confirmed that a significant percentage of contemporary Americans who claim an Evangelical identity rarely attend religious services. In 2008, 16 percent of all self-identified Evangelicals reported "never or seldom" when asked about their church attendance. By 2020, that number was 27 percent. In 2008, a third of self-identified Evangelicals who never attended church claimed to be politically conservative. By 2019, that number approached 50 percent. In addition, growing numbers of Catholics and Muslims now call themselves Evangelical. Apparently, many Americans think that being very religiously engaged and very politically conservative makes one an Evangelical.

Even more troubling, a growing body of research confirms that American Evangelicalism hasn't simply become a political rather than religious identity; to a very significant extent, the American Evangelicals who dominate today's Republican Party are more properly identified as White Christian Nationalists, and they are focused not upon faith but upon the defense of White male Christian privilege.

When it comes to women's rights and the current effort to ban abortions, it is manifestly dishonest to argue that opposition to reproductive choice is grounded in Christian theology. Pastors to whom we have spoken, both those who describe themselves as "pro-life" and those who are "pro-choice," agree that the Bible is silent on the issue. Religious historians have documented that the roots of the anti-abortion movement lie elsewhere. It wasn't until 1979, a full six years after the Court decided Roe v. Wade, that Evangelical leaders, goaded by Paul

Weyrich, seized on abortion as "a rallying-cry to deny President Jimmy Carter a second term." As noted religion scholar Randall Balmer has written, these political figures felt that objecting to abortion would be seen as "more palatable" than what was actually motivating them, which was protection of the segregated schools they had established following the decision in Brown v. Board of Education.

According to Balmer, "Both before and for several years after Roe, evangelicals were overwhelmingly indifferent to the subject, which they considered a "Catholic issue." In 1968, for instance, a symposium sponsored by the Christian Medical Society and *Christianity Today*, the flagship magazine of evangelicalism, refused to characterize abortion as sinful, citing "individual health, family welfare, and social responsibility" as justifications for ending a pregnancy. In 1971, delegates to the Southern Baptist Convention in St. Louis, Missouri, passed a resolution encouraging "Southern Baptists to work for legislation that will allow the possibility of abortion under such conditions as rape, incest, clear evidence of severe fetal deformity, and carefully ascertained evidence of the likelihood of damage to the emotional, mental, and physical health of the mother." The convention, hardly a redoubt of liberal values, reaffirmed that position in 1974, one year after the Roe decision became law, and again in 1976.

It was rightwing anger about civil rights laws that originally motivated the "Right to life" movement. Political actors were savvy enough to recognize that organizing grassroots Evangelicals to defend racial discrimination wouldn't cut it; that they would need a different issue if they wanted to mobilize Evangelical voters on a large scale. Distasteful as that reality is, evidence clearly shows that the Christian Right's political activism, including but not limited to, its opposition to abortion, was largely motivated by a defense of racial segregation, not by religious doctrine.

A lengthy 2022 article from the *Guardian* newspaper of Great Britain reported on the extensive relationships between White supremacist and anti-choice organizations.

> "Explicit white nationalism, and an emphasis on conscripting white women into reproduction, is not a fringe element of the anti-choice movement. Associations between white supremacist groups and anti-abortion forces are robust and longstanding. In addition to Patriot Front, groups like the white nationalist Aryan Nations and the neo-Nazi Traditionalist Worker party have also lent support to the anti-abortion movement. These groups see stopping abortion as part of a broader project to ensure white hegemony in addition to women's subordination. Tim Bishop, of the Aryan Nations, noted that 'Lots of our people join [anti-choice organizations] …

It's part of our Holy War for the pure Aryan race.' That the growing white nationalist movement would be focused on attacking women's rights is maybe to be expected: research has long established that recruitment to the alt-right happens largely among men with grievances against feminism, and that misogyny is usually the first form of rightwing radicalization." [5]

In his decision in *Boggs v. Jackson*, Justice Samuel Alito claimed that reversal of Roe "restores the US to an unbroken tradition of prohibiting abortion on pain of criminal punishment [that] persisted from the earliest days of the common law until 1973." This assertion is deeply dishonest and easily disproved. As historians have exhaustively documented, early American common law (as in Britain) generally permitted abortions until "quickening", or perceptible fetal movement, usually between 16 to 20 weeks into a pregnancy. Connecticut was the first state to ban abortion after quickening, in 1821, which is roughly two centuries after the earliest days of American common law. It wasn't until the 1880s that every U.S. state had some laws restricting abortion, and not until the 1910s that it was criminalized in every state. In the wake of *Dobbs*, social media was awash with examples from 18th- and 19th-century newspapers that clearly refuted Alito's false assertion, sharing examples of midwives and doctors legally advertising abortifacients, Benjamin Franklin's at-home abortion remedies, and accounts of 19th-century doctors performing "therapeutic" (medically necessary) abortions.

As the *Guardian* reported, anti-abortion fervor has not been motivated by the moral or religious beliefs generally cited by anti-choice activists. In fact, the first wave of anti-abortion laws was entangled in arguments about nativism, eugenics, and white supremacy as they dovetailed with a cultural panic that swept the U.S. in the late 19th and early 20th century as a result of the vast changes in American society. This panic was referred to at the time in shorthand as "race suicide."

The increasing traction today of the far-right "great replacement theory", which contends that there is a global conspiracy to replace White people with people of color and Jews and has explicitly motivated white supremacist massacres in the U.S., is often said to have originated with a French novel called *The Camp of the Saints* by Jean Raspail. Published in 1973, the same year that *Roe v. Wade* affirmed American women's rights to reproductive autonomy, it is a dystopian account of "swarthy hordes" of immigrants sweeping in and destroying western civilization. But there were

---

[5] "White nationalists are flocking to the US anti-abortion movement" by Moira Donegan,https://www.theguardian.com/commentisfree/2022/jan/24/whitenat ionalists-are-flocking-to-the-us-anti-abortion-movement [accessed 8/23/22]

many earlier panics over "white extinction", and debates around abortion in the U.S. have been entangled with race panic from the start.

A post on the website of FiveThirtyEight.com put it succinctly: The anti-abortion movement, at its core, has always been about upholding white supremacy." Women's rights were collateral damage.

Of course, religious beliefs, whether seen or unseen, "up front" or latent, rooted in religious belief or racism, are not the only powerful influences shaping American worldviews. American culture also reflects popular understandings of the country's constituent documents—the Declaration of Independence, the Constitution, and the Bill of Rights—documents that are widely venerated (although apparently much less widely read and/or understood). Religion scholars credit the First Amendment's religion clauses, which mandate the separation of church and state, for America's religiosity, a religiosity that flourished here at the same time that Europe was becoming far more secular. The establishment clause of the First Amendment prohibits government from privileging the beliefs and practices of certain religions, while the free exercise clause protects individual beliefs. As a result of the operation of those two clauses (for which the phrase "separation of church and state" is shorthand), the United States has nurtured a wide diversity of religions, including numerous denominations within the country's dominant Christianity. As the foregoing descriptions illustrate, there is no uniformity among them on the status of women or on the extent of female agency or on the permissibility of birth control or abortion. What we do know about religion's influence on the status of women (globally as well as within the United States) is simple: the lower the level of religious affiliation and fervor, the higher the level of gender equality.

A Constitutional U-Turn

In addition to the First Amendment's prohibition against legislating religious doctrine, for the past fifty years Americans have relied upon a constitutional doctrine known as substantive due process, often called the "right to privacy." That doctrine has strengthened the conviction of most Americans that certain "intimate" individual decisions, including one's choice of sexual partners or the decision to use contraception, are none of the government's business.

The right to privacy was explicitly recognized in a 1965 case titled *Griswold v. Connecticut.* The Court was considering the constitutionality of a Connecticut law prohibiting the use of birth control by married couples. (The law also prohibited doctors from prescribing and pharmacists from selling contraceptives.) William O. Douglas's majority opinion reflected the logic of its conclusion. He wrote,

"Would we allow the police to search the sacred precincts of marital bedrooms for telltale signs of the use of contraceptives? The very idea is repulsive to the notions of privacy surrounding the marriage relationship."

The majority recognized that a right to personal autonomy was necessary to the enforcement of several of the amendments, which Douglas noted would be difficult or impossible to respect without the implicit recognition of such an underlying right. In a concurrence, Justice Arthur Goldberg found that same right in the Ninth Amendment, and Justices Byron White and John Marshall Harlan II argued that privacy is protected by the due process clause of the Fourteenth Amendment— hence the doctrinal title "substantive due process." Wherever it resided, in a "penumbra" or the 14th Amendment, a majority of the Justices have agreed on its presence and importance.

Procedural due process protects Americans' right to a fair process—a fair trial or other governmental proceeding. *Substantive* due process distinguishes between decisions that the government has the legitimate authority to make and decisions which must be left to each individual. In the fifty years since *Griswold*, the recognition that the U.S. Constitution protects personal autonomy and respects the right of each individual to self-determination has powerfully influenced American culture. Much of the anger over the Supreme Court's decision in *Dobbs* can be traced to shock over Justice Alito's assault on what most Americans had come to consider a bedrock principle.

Simply stated, the principle is that government has the right—indeed the obligation—to intervene when a person's behaviors are harming people who haven't consented to that harm. (Mask mandates to protect public health are an example.) Otherwise, the government must leave us alone. Secular and religiously tolerant Americans who had dismissed warnings about growing fundamentalist assaults on that principle, confident that their right to self-determination was secure, reacted to the conservative Christian overtones in *Dobbs*, justifying an invasion of that right, with predictable shock.

As the foregoing discussion has made clear, different religions and different denominations within those religions have very different beliefs about women and procreation, and what amounts to the Court's elevation of a particular version of Christianity has engendered an enormous and negative reaction. Survey research has confirmed that a majority of Americans, including a majority of religiously affiliated Americans, disagree with the Court's decision and are even more opposed to emerging efforts to make access to contraception difficult or impossible. Large numbers of Americans see the overturning of Roe and cases like *Hobby Lobby* in defense of so-called "religious freedom" as part of an escalating war on women.

Chapter Three: Cause and Effect

Morton J. Marcus

Cause-and-effect is a delightful concept. Release an uncooked egg from a window on the twentieth floor of a building, directly above a concrete platform and you have the very strong probability of a splattered egg. It's fun and comforting to know what will happen. Although some persons ascribe to strong probabilities of cause-and-effect relationships in economic matters, they are not writing this chapter. Here the view is that nominal causes exist, but real causes are often impossible to determine.

So-called laws in economics (raise prices and less will be sold) are statements of likelihood, subject to deviations determined by factors most lawgivers would prefer not to consider. *Ceteris paribus* (all else being the same) needs to remain in the freshman classroom and not be heard in the Congressional hearing room where complexity must be understood.

Many causes are best described as enabling or facilitating factors. The first U.S. women's rights conference in Seneca Falls, New York, might not have been feasible in 1838 but was enabled in 1848 by the development of railway service across the state in the intervening decade. The lower cost and greater convenience of transportation in 1848 did not give rise to the women's movement but possibly contributed to its initiation.

Likewise, data offered up by respected statistical agencies of the federal government (the Census Bureau, the Bureau of Economic Analysis (BEA), and the Bureau of Labor Statistics (BLS)) are estimates based on careful collection practices, solid belief in statistical theory, artful algorithms, and occasionally audited reports of private and public entities. They are not facts in the sense that we believe *ex post* temperature and wind velocity measurements to be—but neither are they falsifications for political or ideological purposes. Whatever imperfections exist in those data are under ritualized professional scrutiny. Frequent revisions (as with the BEA estimates of Gross Domestic Product (GDP) or the BLS labor market data) are the result of incorporating late reporting and necessary adjustments made possible by more complete data at a later time, known as annual benchmarking.

Other data difficulties arise from the necessity to revise familiar categories to accommodate new concepts and features of the world about which we wish to make decisions. Newspapers were previously included under printing and publishing in the manufacturing sector. Process was the determining factor. In today's world, newspapers are products of the information sector based on their content rather than their mode of distribution.

The Census Bureau asks questions that may not seem pertinent to a book on the progress of women. For example, in the past the Bureau asked whether a housing unit had a radio but now tracks households with or without internet access. These data, however, give us an indication of the ability of the "woman-stuck-at-home" to keep current with the world. When something can be presumed ubiquitous, its presence is not needed on a questionnaire.

Funding and politics can limit or extend data. When Congress balked at a presumed "invasion of privacy," the Census Bureau eliminated many questions previously collected on the long form of the Decennial Census. Instead, they substituted the collection of additional data from annual and ongoing samples.

Women's public involvement in paid labor and policies related to it in America dates back to 1765 (and is well-illustrated in an excellent chronology of women in the workplace).[6] World War I introduced many women to the paid labor market for the first time. As the safety of female workers became a concern, the Department of Labor began collecting data on the numbers of women employed. In 1920, the department also initiated the Women's Bureau to study policy questions related specifically to the employment of women. As data accumulates, greater detail is provided by panels of experts whose classifications and distinctions are written into law and subsequently assigned for collection. This has been the case with the data on poverty, grandparents rearing children, and women.

In the following sections, we examine data concerning women and the economy. But first we'll look back at the trajectory of women's legal and economic advancement.

Enabling Factors

Traditional histories trace the beginning of the women's movement in the United States to a conference at Seneca Falls, approximately twenty-five miles west of Syracuse, on July 19 and 20, 1848. A primary goal of the movement, the abolition of coverture, which began the process of women's liberation from medieval serfdom, started in the latter part of the 18th century. Coverture was the English (and hence American) legal practice of declaring that a woman was under the protection of her

---

[6] "History of Women in the Workplace" by Joni Sweet, https://stacker.com/business-economy/history-women-workplace [accessed 10/28/22]

husband or some other male relative and, as such, could neither own nor make decisions about property. In effect, married women did not exist as legal beings separate from their husbands. Upon marriage, any prior agreements about property were void. The husband held all rights to property and exercised all powers with respect to the use of wealth, whether originally his or his wife's. Women were expected to be known by their husbands' family name or title. This practice largely persists. Only recently have women been able to get credit in their own names and maintain social relations without being Mrs. Somebody.

Coverture laws were dismantled one state at a time, beginning in Mississippi in 1839, New York in 1848, and continuing elsewhere into the 1880s.[7] As the legal disabilities of women were being partially removed, females began the protracted process of becoming persons in their own right.

This advance was nurtured by the Declaration of Independence, the subsequent American and French Revolutions, and the dissemination of opinions like Mary Wollstonecraft's *A Vindication of the Rights of Woman* (1797) which argued for an education of women equivalent to that of men. (One revolutionary man, Aaron Burr, Jefferson's Vice President, was an ardent admirer of Wollstonecraft's thought throughout his turbulent career.)

While political philosophers struggled with concepts of democracy, James Hargreaves in England patented the spinning Jenny (1770), which could control eight spools of thread simultaneously, greatly improving productivity of home spinners. A year earlier, Richard Arkwright patented the water frame, powered by fast running water and producing a stronger product than the spinning Jenny. Because of its power source and large size, the water frame was not adapted for home production. As factories for this mechanism were built, spinning and spinners (men, women, and children) moved from domestic sites into the factories of the Industrial Revolution. During the ensuing decade, Samuel Crompton brought together the spinning Jenny and the water frame; his spinning mule could produce fine and coarse thread on a thousand spindles controlled by a single operator.[8]

These advances in spinning thread made cotton and wool less costly to produce and more valuable in the marketplace. In America, ambitious farmer-landowners were ignoring patent laws by developing and adapting

---

[7] "Coverture" https://www.britannica.com/event/Married-Womens-Property-Acts-United-States-1839 [accessed 11/4/22]

[8] "Brian Duignan, Inventors and Inventions of the Industrial Revolution"

https://www.britannica.com/list/inventors-and-inventions-of-the-industrial-revolution [accessed 11/11/22]

Eli Whitney's cotton gin (1794). This machine, which separated seeds from fiber, reduced the need for long, tedious hours of labor and made cotton the major crop of the southern states. As the cost of cotton fell, the demand by northern and European fabric producers increased. Likewise, southern farmers, responding to the increase in demand for cotton, planted more acres of cotton and needed more slaves to tend and harvest the mature plants. Ironically, a labor-saving device ended up increasing demand for more labor in the form of slaves and augmenting the rationale for the southern economic system.

With the U.S. Constitution[9] ending the legal importation of slaves in 1808 and the increased value of slave labor in the cotton fields, breeding slaves became more important to slave owners and traders. These conditions strengthened opposition to slavery and its cruelty for enslaved women.

Thus, spinning machines and the cotton gin contributed to the abolitionist fervor that eventually paved part of the path toward women's liberation.

Whitney's next innovation was the use of interchangeable parts (1797) in the manufacture of rifles. When identical parts were employed in the manufacture of goods, costs were reduced and quality improved. This innovation lessened the role of craftsmanship and introduced mass production. One level of skilled labor was replaced by a different set of skills necessary to work with high volume machinery. Higher volumes of products led to greater profits as well as lower prices to consumers. For the displaced workers, however, it often meant a loss of identity and status along with a loss of income.

Standardization enabled improvements in the lives of millions around the world. Among the newly mass-produced items was an entire set of goods that differentially favored women. They included the sewing machine, the wringer-washer, the apple-corer-slicer, the meat grinder—any product that could be used by hand or foot power on a scale sufficiently small for the home. Less effort and more precision improved tasks usually performed by women by reducing the time and effort need-ed for those tasks.

Post-Civil War America saw wealth accumulated by entrepreneurs in new industries. Land ownership, which had been a major source of wealth, declined in consequence during this era. Financiers and industrialists were in the ascendancy. Innovation and capital development led to the displacement of a segment of labor for generations, with the major rewards going to the innovators and the capital owners. Just as in the case of the

---

[9] This information can be found in Article I, Section 9.

cotton gin, the invention of labor-saving devices for the home would often benefit one group at the expense of another.

After the Civil War, increased industrialization led to the creation of larger firms and a burgeoning middle class of professional and managerial workers. Many households sent their laundry out to be washed by female workers and their garments to be tailored by others who were among the poorest of the community. The advent of the wringer -washing machine and sewing machine for the home adversely affected the income of laundresses and seamstresses when newly middle-class homemakers added laundry and tailoring to their tasks. At the same time, however, the sewing machine, washers and dryers, vacuum cleaners, refrigerators, and the multitude of home cooking devices could generate higher incomes for entrepreneurial lower-income workers if they had the capital to invest in them. Similarly, tasks previously assigned to servants or out-sourced could be performed by the homemaker more quickly and with less effort, leaving her to take paid employment or devote more time to civic and charitable causes if she had invested in these capital goods.

The bicycle was one mass-produced item that had revolutionary implications for women in the latter part of the 19th century. Men rode bikes to get to and from work, for recreation, for sport, and as part of the job (couriers), but women found the bicycle gave them independence. They no longer had to hitch a horse to the cart. With the improved roadways of the 1880s and '90s, women could move about the community with greater ease, go to and from work, attend programs, visit with friends, and conspire against domestic oppression all on their own.

Bicycling brought forth fierce arguments on women's health and the benefits/costs of engaging in such activities. Frances Elizabeth Willard's book *A Wheel Within A Wheel* (1895) argued for riding for health and sociability. (As President of the Women's Christian Temperance Union, Willard pedaled her way to upbraid imbibers.) The staid suffragette Susan B. Anthony (1820-1906) is quoted as saying in 1896, "Bicycling... has done more to emancipate women than anything else in the world."[10] So revolutionary was the woman on a bicycle that even the clothes she wore for riding became a contest between convenience and convention. Billowing bloomers were adopted for their practicality while criticized for flaunting impiety in dress.

Also prominent in the advancement of women during this era were the telephone, newspapers, and magazines. As reading became more prevalent and media directed attention to the female audience, the printed word

---

[10] "Pedaling the Path to Freedom: American Women on Bicycles" https://www. womenshistory.org/articles/pedaling-path-freedom [accessed11/11/22]

opened the world to millions. The telephone, a luxury item at first, became a primary instrument of communication, particularly for women at home.

Among the many enablers of the women's movement, and perhaps the most significant, was the electrification of the home. The aforementioned vacuum cleaner, washing machine, dryer, dishwasher, hair dryer, refrigerator, and radio were followed by the microwave oven, TV, and computer. These were reliable and relatively inexpensive life-changing home appliances. In addition, electricity meant the house could be better lit than by candlelight, oil lamp, or gas fixtures. This effectively lengthened the day and provided more flexibility in managing the time available for domestic chores and outside opportunities. Electricity in the home was safer and healthier than open fires. It also made learning at home more convenient. Electricity used for street lighting made the streets safer for women, enabling them to engage in after dark or pre-dawn activities.

The impact of consumer technologies on women's emancipation was immense, but labor-saving devices weren't the only contributors to the changing social status of women. Changes in American law were equally significant.

Title IX

Among the under-appreciated factors fueling social and economic advances in U.S. gender equity in the past two hundred years was the passage in 1972 of Title IX. *Equal Play*, a detailed, scholarly volume, provides the background of Title IX, the process of its adoption, the various backlashes against it, efforts to change it, and how it has been administered.[11] As several commentators observed on the law's fiftieth anniversary, "In 1972 no one dreamed a dry, 37-word clause tucked inside new education legislation would reshape women's sports forever."[12]

These are the 37 words: *"No person in the United States shall, on the basis of sex, be excluded from participation in, be denied the benefits of, or be subjected to discrimination under any education program or activity receiving federal financial assistance."* [13]

---

[11] Nancy Hogshead-Makar and Andrew Zimbalist, eds., *Equal Play, Title IX, and Social Change* (Temple University Press: Philadelphia, 2007).

[12] Maggie Mertens,"The Pursuit of Equal Play," *Sports Illustrated*, June 2022, p.27.

[13] Hogshead-Makar and Zimbalist., op cit, 67. See Section 901 (a) of Title IX of the Education Amendments of 1972

Besides questioning the propriety and need for Title IX, opponents were particularly concerned that women's collegiate sports would divert funds and physical resources from existing men's athletic programs. Senator Birch Bayh (D-Indiana), one of chief proponents of Title IX, made a prophetic statement in 1974 at a hearing on a pernicious amendment to Title IX offered by Senator John Tower (R-Texas), Bayh said:

> "It is unbelievable to me that sports programs so steeped in tradition as most of our big-ten schools are suddenly going to disintegrate or even be seriously damaged or even slightly damaged by permitting the women to attend these same fine institutions and have an equal opportunity to participate in athletic programs and programs of physical education."[14]

Extensive media coverage in 2022 noted the progress made and yet to be made by Title IX in sports. However, most failed to give much attention to the cultural advances far beyond sports that can be traced to its passage. There is no question that the path to equity and equality for women in collegiate sports has not been smooth. When student-athlete Amy Cohen entered Brown University in 1988, she found that the women gymnasts did not have their own trainer, laundry service for workout uniforms, accommodation for use of the gym, or out-of-town travel arrangements equal to those in men's sports.[15] As recently as 2022, "Olivia Pichardo, a freshman utility player and walk-on at Brown, became the first woman to make an active NCAA Division I baseball varsity roster.... According to the non-profit organization Baseball for All, nearly 20 women have made college baseball rosters. Pichardo is the first to do so at the NCAA Division I level."[16]

Title IX offers opportunities for women to participate in collegiate sports. But there had been significant women in sports in earlier years. Margaret Abbot at the Paris Olympics of 1900 won the golf competition for women.[17] Perhaps the most outstanding female competitor of the 20th century was Babe Didrikson Zaharias, a 1932 Olympic medalist in track

---

[14] Ibid., p. 63.

[15] Ibid., p.140.

[16] "Brown adds first woman to active D-I varsity baseball roster" https://www.espn.com/college-sports/story/_/id/35076550/ brown-adds-first-woman-active-d1-baseball-varsity-roster_[accessed 11/3/22]

[17] Abbott was unaware of her participation and victory in the disorganized Olympics that year. "Margaret Abbott: A Study Break" https://www.britannica.com/topic/A-Study-Break-1367944_[accessed 11/3/22]

and field, a renowned golfer, and accomplished basketball player.[18] Althea Gibson dominated women's tennis in the late 1950s, winning the French Open (1956), Wimbledon (1957–58), and U.S. Open (1957–58) singles titles. In the Munich Olympic games of 1972, U.S. women won 11 of 14 swim meets. A year later, tennis star Billie Jean King defeated an over-the-hill Bobby Riggs, denying the latter's claim to universal male superiority in sports.

Most of these achievements were made at non-collegiate, individual competitions. Title IX opened the door to less stellar players in team sports. In the early days, during the '70s and into the '80s, the male-oriented media focused on the sexual attraction of female competitors. In some cases it still does, particularly in volleyball where slender, bikini-wearing women prance for the TV cameras.

Over the course of two generations, the effect of Title IX has drawn millions of young women into competitive sports. This has brought forth proud parents and grandparents to accept participation from softball to lacrosse. The impact of Title IX has been so significant because Americans are addicted to sports. Sports champions become icons and their branded products sell. The adulation realized by Venus and Serena Williams, winners of thirty Grand Slam singles tennis tournaments, is a recent example. In Serena's case, especially, competitive conquests have led to commercial success.

It may not be stretching the point too far to claim that acceptance in sports is a forerunner to success in business and politics for otherwise denigrated groups. Title IX gave women an important base from which to extend their struggle for recognition in all fields of endeavor—and provided important cultural support for the other significant changes to discriminatory laws referenced in Chapter 2.

Organization of a Movement

The changes desired by millions of people burst forth in the remarkable year of 1848. Political change in Europe, starting with the French overthrow of the Bourbon emperor in that year, stimulated revolts, riots, and repression in other European nations.[19] In America, dissatisfaction

[18] "Babe Didrikson Zaharias" https://www.britannica.com/biography/Babe-Didrikson-Zaharias [accessed 11/1/22]

[19] "Modern History Sourcebook: Carl Schurz: A Look Back at 1848, 1907 https://sourcebooks.fordham.edu/mod/1848schurz.asp [accessed 11/11/23]

with the Mexican War (also known as "A Wicked War")[20] and, with the hardly forgotten Jacksonian recession of the 1830s, stirred religious revival, nativist movements, and labor organization. These were superseded in fervor by the antislavery ferment that would erupt in the 1850s. Underlying this social turbulence was a quiet revolution that would bring about a measure of female emancipation, political recognition, and economic advancement. Empowerment, however, was won slowly and aided by technological developments that, in many cases, were differentially advantageous to women.

The women's rights convention at Seneca Falls brought three hundred people to that small town located on the Auburn and Rochester rail line.[21] Completed in 1841, this early New York State railroad was an enabling technology for the women's movement. Ten years earlier, a gathering of such significance and magnitude might not have been possible. In the spirit and style of the *Declaration of Independence*, human rights activist and convention organizer Elizabeth Cady Stanton proclaimed the now celebrated "Declaration of Sentiments" along with other attendees:

> *"The history of mankind is a history of repeated injuries and usurpations on the part of man toward woman, having in direct object the establishment of an absolute tyranny over her.*
>
> *_He has never permitted her to exercise her inalienable right to the elective franchise.*
>
> *_He has compelled her to submit to laws, in the formation of which she had no voice.*
>
> *_He has withheld from her rights which are given to the most ignorant and degraded men—both natives and foreigners.*
>
> *_Having deprived her of this first right of a citizen, the elective franchise, thereby leaving her without representation in the halls of legislation, he has oppressed her on all sides.*
>
> *_He has made her, if married, in the eye of the law, civilly dead.*
>
> *_He has taken from her all right in property, even to the wages she earns.*
>
> *_He has made her, morally, an irresponsible being, as she can commit many crimes, with impunity, provided they be done in the presence of her husband. In the covenant of marriage, she is compelled to promise obedience to her husband,*

---

[20] Amy S. Greenberg, A Wicked War, Polk, Clay, Lincoln, and the 1846 U.S. Invasion of Mexico (New York: Alfred A. Knopf, 2012) explores public opposition to the war, the role of women, and the mood for disrupting authoritarian government.

[21] "Railroads and Trolley Lines of Geneva N.Y." Text of a lecture by Bud Smith for the Geneva Historical Society, 17 February 1987. http://fglk.railfan.net/history.html [accessed 11/2/22].

he becoming, to all intents and purposes, her master—the law giving him power to deprive her of her liberty, and to administer chastisement.

_He has so framed the laws of divorce, as to what shall be the proper causes of divorce; in case of separation, to whom the guardianship of the children shall be given, as to be wholly regardless of the happiness of women—the law, in all cases, going upon the false supposition of the supremacy of man, and giving all power into his hands.

_After depriving her of all rights as a married woman, if single and the owner of property, he has taxed her to support a government which recognizes her only when her property can be made profitable to it.

_He has monopolized nearly all the profitable employments, and from those she is permitted to follow, she receives but a scanty remuneration.

_He closes against her all the avenues to wealth and distinction, which he considers most honorable to himself. As a teacher of theology, medicine, or law, she is not known.

_He has denied her the facilities for obtaining a thorough education—all colleges being closed against her.

_He allows her in Church as well as State, but a subordinate position, claiming Apostolic authority for her exclusion from the ministry, and with some exceptions, from any public participation in the affairs of the Church.

_He has created a false public sentiment, by giving to the world a different code of morals for men and women, by which moral delinquencies which exclude women from society, are not only tolerated but deemed of little account in man.

_He has usurped the prerogative of Jehovah himself, claiming it as his right to assign for her a sphere of action, when that belongs to her conscience and her God.

_He has endeavored, in every way that he could, to destroy her confidence in her own powers, to lessen her self-respect, and to make her willing to lead a dependent and abject life."

Such was the passion and militancy of this "Declaration" that only one hundred (68 women and 32 men) of the three hundred said to be present signed the document in its final form. For a nation swelling with pride as it vanquished the Mexicans and enriched itself by annexing new territories, some felt this litany of injustices beat the drums of a war against men. However, the war subsequently fought was a regional conflict against slavery. Metaphorically, that war was against a house divided, rather than a battle within each house.

The Civil War would stimulate American industry at the same time that it killed or maimed thousands of combatants and destroyed the physical capital and spirit of the South. The productivity of steam-driven farm equipment eventually outweighed the loss of labor. In fact, as the federal government stepped away from supporting a large army, the nation's farms were exhibiting a labor surplus. At the end of the Civil War, the North found itself with better rail and road routes, massive new firms, and networks operating as corporations rather than as sole-proprietorships or limited partnerships. While the South licked its wounds and became embittered, wed to "Lost Cause" fictions about its past, the North, without yielding its racism, adjusted to the industrial, urban age.

With diminished resources and limited opportunities, Southern women played a very small role in the women's movement. In the North, industry had been drawing single women out of the home from the 1820s forward. This was part of the abandonment of "farming out" work to peasant households on tenant farms. More prevalent in the British Isles than in the U.S., where distances were a deterrent, women worked from home for the nascent cloth industry, spinning, weaving, and sewing garments. Once these functions were transferred to more efficient, more uniform factories, women, girls, and boys followed, finding employment in those industrial locales.

Many of those sites were sweatshops, unsafe and unregulated. New York's Triangle Shirtwaist Factory fire in 1911, in which 146 workers were killed, became a stimulus for reform and the introduction of safety and other labor rules. Ironically, many of the deceased were Jewish and Italian immigrant girls who worked twelve-hour days making a product viewed as personifying the modern woman.[22]

With many women entering the labor market during World War I and then leaving when the wartime need expired, the working conditions of women became more evident and of greater public concern. In what remained of a chivalrous era, the protection of women workers became a priority. In recognition of the importance of their wartime efforts and the conditions of their employment, the U.S. Department of Labor formed the Women's Bureau in 1921 to study and provide information relevant to the status of women in the labor force. Much of the data collected by and for the BLS now addresses precisely issues of concern to women.

Just as World War I changed the view of women in the workforce, the concept of the total economy was being updated. How can we capture economic activity in a single, uniform measure? The 1920s, like the post-Civil War period, were years of dramatic surges of growth and decline. The 1930s saw little growth, with extraordinary decline and hardship. In 1937,

---

[22] "What is a Shirtwaist?" https://www.pbs.org/wgbh/americanexperience /features /triangle-fire-what-shirtwaist/ [accessed 11/12/22]

Simon Kuznets[23] introduced the notion of the GDP, which has become the worldwide standard for assessing economic performance.

The labor of women in business and government would be included in the GDP, but what about the work they did at home, the tasks of homemaking, raising children, and caring for others? Those non-market activities were not included in the measurement and valuation of economic activities. And where we do not have measurement, our society tends to neglect and negate value. With a changed perception of domestic work, the Bureau of Economic Analysis has now begun producing estimates for the value of work at home. Recognition and information are another vital, enabling factor in the progress of women. This subject will be treated in more detail in the following chapter.

---

[23] The National Bureau of Economic Research promoted the concept of Gross Domestic Product and presented the first estimates of GDP to Congress in "National Income, 1929-35."

Chapter Four: Paths of Progress

Morton J. Marcus

Population

The number and characteristics of women in American life have been in flux since the founding of the nation. Hence data from the Census Bureau becomes the foundation of understanding the magnitudes and issues in successive periods of time. In 2021, the United States had 166.2 million resident females in the population compared to 162.8 million males. In Figure 4.1 the age distribution of these women is shown on the left scale of the graph. Women as a percent of the total population at each age level is shown on the right scale. At all ages below 45 years, females are slightly in the minority. Beyond that age, females quickly become dominant, reaching close to 64% of those 85 and older. Remember, these data are for a single year, a point in time. Later in this discussion, we'll see the trend over time is moving favorably for men.

Figure 4.1: Number and Percent of Females in the U.S. Population, 2021

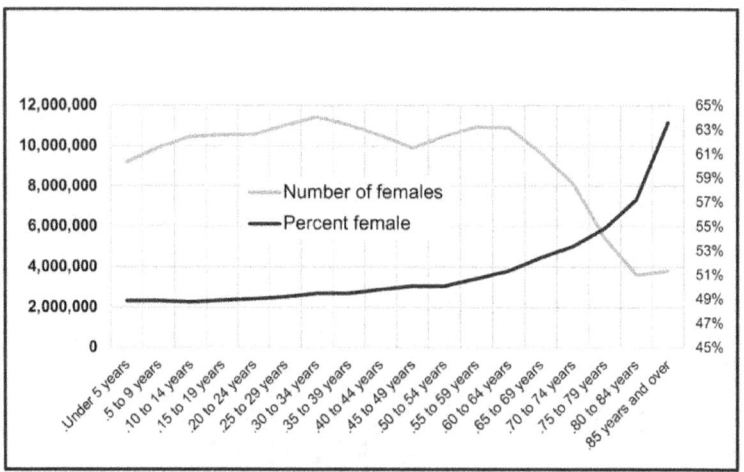

Source: U.S. Census Bureau

There are eighteen age groups shown in Figure 4.1, each corresponding to a set of years at which that cohort was born. Those under 5 years old in 2021 were born in 2017 or later. Those 85 and older were born in 1936 or earlier. Half of the female population of the U.S. currently is under age 45, that is, born in 1981 or later.

By now, the Baby Boomers are a shrinking group. The youngest are 60 or older, born from 1946 to 1961. They account for just over 17% of the total female population. The next cohort, ages 45 to 59 (born 1962 to 1976) represent 19% of females. The largest cohort in 2021 were those 25 to 39 years old (born 1982 to 1996), totaling 20% of females. Mortality will reduce each of those cohorts as they progress through life.

Attention in the years ahead will be focused on the middle and older cohorts and their impact on Medicare, Medicaid, and Social Security. But more serious attention needs to be given to those under age 30. As Figure 4.1 indicates, there are fewer females in each cohort below age 30. The same is the case for males of comparable ages. This situation promises a shrinking pool of workers to support those in the older groups. On the upside, it can mean less competition for jobs and resources in the decades ahead, with less economic growth from sheer numbers and less potential ecological damage.

The tendency for females to survive to older ages is of long standing as shown in Figure 4.2. Since 1900, females have had a greater life expectancy than males. World War I and the flu pandemic of 1918-19 caused a temporary decline in life expectancy for both sexes.

Figure 4.2: Life Expectancy at Birth, U.S. Females and Males, 1900 – 2018

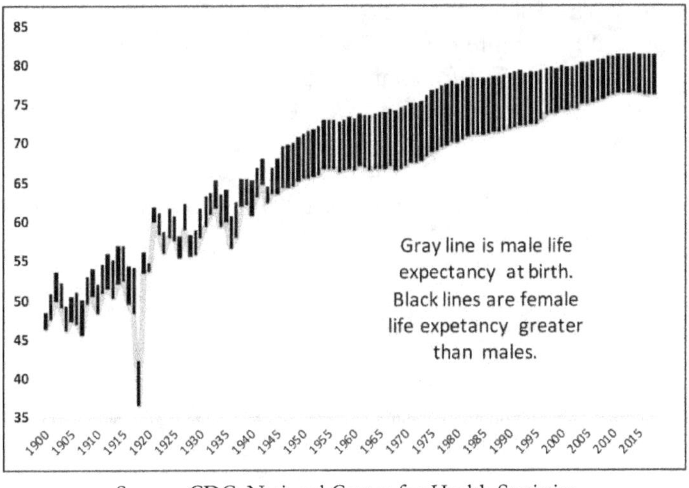

Gray line is male life expectancy at birth. Black lines are female life expectancy greater than males.

Source: CDC: National Center for Health Statistics

The life expectancy of females and males was 48.3 years and 46.3 years, respectively, in 1900. By 2018 female life expectancy advanced by 32.9 years to 81.2; for males, the advancement was more modest at 29.9 years to 76.2. The starting differential in 1900 favoring females was two years and grew to five years in 2018. As we shall see, this differential has several causal factors and implications for the future. As ever, decennial U.S. Census data tell many stories. The first census in 1790 reported data for more than the number of states (13) admitted to the Union at that time. Data were also provided as part of the U.S. total for Vermont (admitted in 1791) and Kentucky (1792), as well as Maine, which was not admitted to the Union until 1820.

That 1790 Census provided a total count for these 16 states in the following groups:

Free white males of age 16 and up	807,094
Free white males under 16 years	791,850
Free white female	1,541,263
Other free persons	51,150
Slaves	649,280
Total	3,893,635

That these numbers do not add up precisely to the total shown was probably the origin of the expression, "Pretty good for government work." Of note is the lack of attention to the ages of the "Free white females" and the absence of information about the sex of the "Other free persons" and the "Slaves." The 1820 Census, however, presented minimal detail about the age of the "Free white females" and the sex of the "Slaves." Given this *progress*, it became possible to obtain the total number of males and females counted as shown for 1820 and subsequent census years from which we derive Figure 4.3.

Figure 4.3: U.S. Sex Ratios per 1,000 Persons, 1820 – 2020

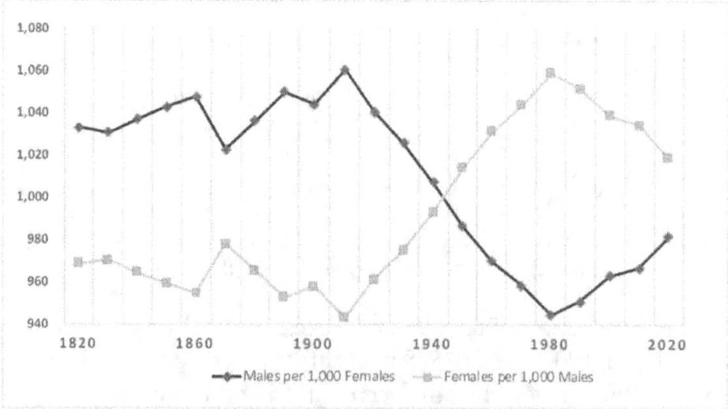

Source: U.S. Census Bureau

Certain events may be observed in these data. The Civil War between 1860 and 1870 had a marked effect on the ratios as so many men died in that conflict. With that exception, the trend is clearly upward for the ratio of Men to Women until 1910. However, from 1910 to 1980 the trend was reversed with Women in the ascendency.

What was going on here? We may speculate that two factors were at work. First, immigrants, from times immemorial, have been Men entering the new land, often as warriors or workers. After that date, we might have seen not only more women entering the country, but certainly major improvements in women's health. This second factor cut the deaths of women during and following pregnancy. It also contributed to reduced infant and child mortality. This latter benefit is frequently associated with fewer pregnancies in a virtuous cycle.

Certain events shaped these data. In the decade between 1860 and 1870, five years of civil war had a marked effect on the ratios because so many men died in that conflict. With that exception, the trend is clearly upward for the ratio of men to women until 1910. However, from 1910 to 1980 the trend was reversed with women in ascendency. Thereafter, we see the two ratios converging.

What was going on here? This ascendency in the ratio of women to men is likely to be a function of several factors, including increased urbanization, more educated women, and greater household income. In addition, at least two other factors were at work: immigration and improved health care.

The trend of legal migration to the U.S. seen in Figure 4.4 is clearly upward, interrupted by World Wars I and II, as well as the Immigration Act of 1924, and the Immigration Act of 1990—both restricting the flow of immigrants.

Immigrants entering the U.S. have historically been men who come as warriors or workers and are followed by women and other family members. This might account for the increasing proportion of men up to 1910.

From the 1920s to '70s, we might have seen more women than men entering the country as families were reunited. But major improvements in women's health during and following pregnancy also contributed to women's increasing ratio in the population. Yet what has caused the resumption of an increase of the proportion of men with the concomitant decrease in the proportion of women since 1980? Though we do not know with certainty, the increase might be related to a reduction in male mortality related to specific occupations (e.g., black lung disease) and behavioral modifications (e.g., reduced smoking), while heart disease and diabetes might be taking more female lives than previously.

Figure 4.4: Number of Legal Migrants to the U.S., 1820 – 2020 (5 Year Moving Average)

Source: U.S. Census Bureau, Historical Statistical Abstract

The combination of these many factors has resulted in women accounting for more than half of the U.S. population across most of the non-Hispanic groups shown in Figure 4.5. Among Hispanic populations, the results are reversed, likely due to ongoing and recently increased immigration from Mexico, Central America, and South America.

Figure 4.5: Women as a Percent of the Total Population by Race and Ethnicity, 2021

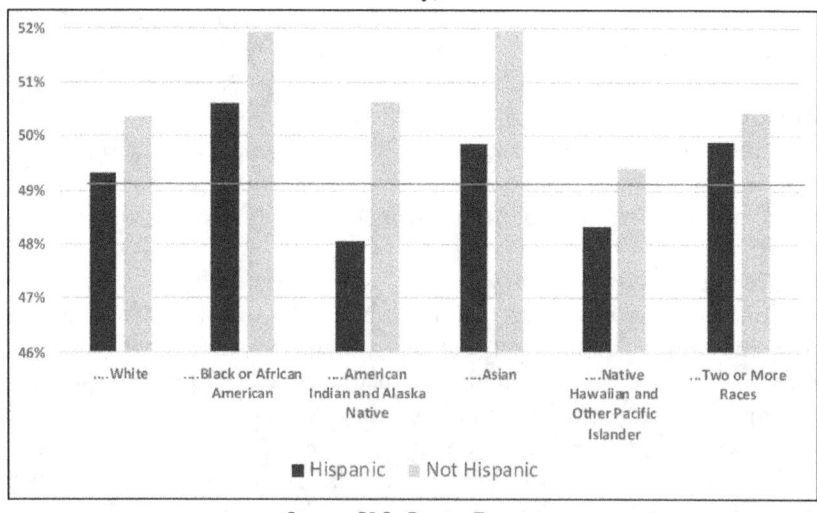

Source: U.S. Census Bureau

A crucial factor in the progress of women in American society has been education. In 1940, 35% of women had five to eight years of schooling, more than any other level of attainment (Figure 4.6). Women who had completed four or more years of college (5%) were fewer than those who had less than five years of elementary school. The progression of attainment is clearly evident in Figure 4.6. In 1960 and 1970, four years of high school was the most common level of schooling. By 1980, the percentage of women with some college was rising. The 2020 pattern shows progressively increasing levels of schooling; women with four or more years of college were the dominant group at 46%.

Figure 4.6: Percent of Women Age 25+ with Specified Years of Schooling, 1940 – 2020

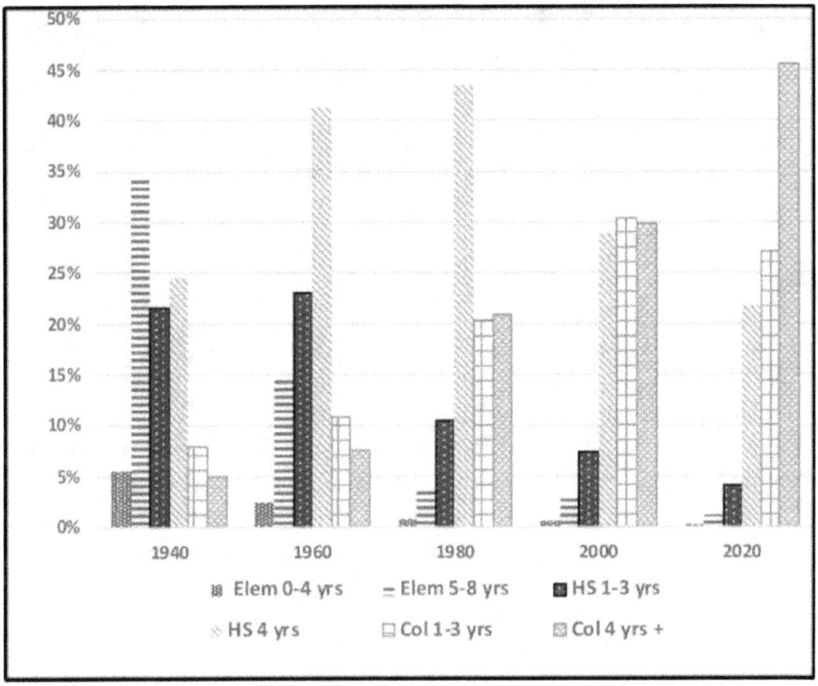

Source: U.S. Census Bureau

By 2021, women 55 years or older accounted for more than half of all persons at each of six levels of schooling attainment (Figure 4.7). Further, as we climb the education ladder, women are more widely represented. Thus, all three age groups make up 50% or more of both college levels. Notably, the youngest cohort of women, those 25 to 34, are most highly represented in the group with four or more years of college.

Figure 4.7: Women as a Percent of All Persons Age 25+ with Years of Schooling, 2021

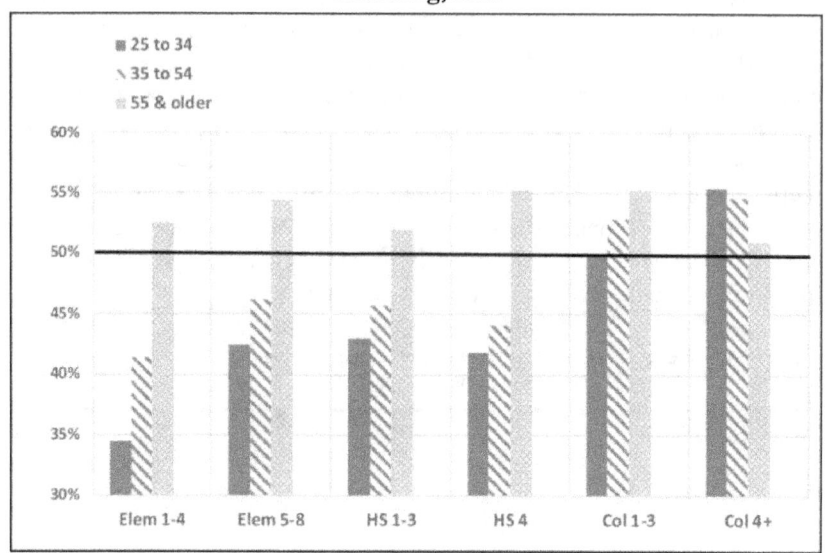

Source: U.S. Census Bureau

Working

Before we proceed, it is worth noting that much of the data that follows on working, wages, and occupations refers to the civilian noninstitutional population. This means that people in prisons, mental institutions, and homes for the aged, in addition to those on active military duty, are excluded. In data concerning the labor force, the relevant population is age 16 and older. With regard to education, the relevant population is age 25 and older.

In 2020, the United States had 230,000 women in the active-duty military. They are not considered to be part of the labor force, although they are employed full time. Women constituted 17% of the enlisted personnel and 19% of the officers.[24]

---

[24] U.S. Department of Defense, 2020 Demographics, Profile of the Military Community. https://download.militaryonesource.mil/12038/MOS/Reports/2020-demographics-report.pdf [12/1/22]

Table 4.1: The Gender Composition of the U.S. Military

Service	Gender	Change 2000 to 2020	
Army	Men	1,496	0.40%
	Women	1,310	1.80%
Navy	Men	-44,438	-14.00%
	Women	19,063	37.70%
Marines	Men	2,284	1.40%
	Women	5,719	54.80%
Air Force	Men	-25,112	-8.80%
	Women	3,401	5.10%
Total	Men	-65,770	-5.60%
	Women	29,493	
		Number	Percentage

Source: U.S. Department of Defense

Between 2000 and 2020, the U.S. armed forces were selectively reducing the numbers of men in the Navy and the Air Force (Table 4.1). However, women increased in number and share in each service. While the number of men declined by 65,800 (-5.6%), women increased by 29,500 (14.7%), boosting their share in the armed services from 14.6% to 17.6%. The 230,000 women in the armed forces were a small number compared to the 69.2 million women employed in the civilian economy in 2020. Since 1948, as the U.S. economy has transitioned from wartime production to peacetime activities at home and reconstruction abroad, the number of women at work quadrupled from 16.6 million to a pre-Covid peak of 74.1 million in 2019. (The dotted line and the right scale in Figure 4.8)

Figure 4.8: Women in the Labor Force, 1948 – 2000

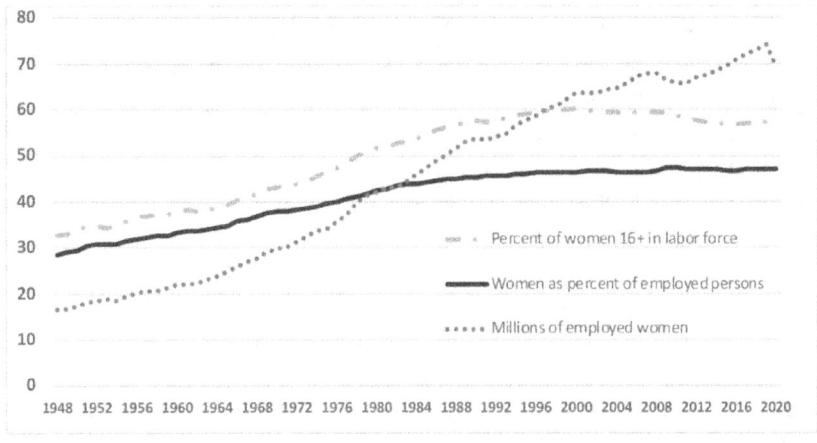

Source: U.S. Bureau of Labor Statistics

This dramatic rise in women's employment was arguably the most significant economic change in America since the end of World War II. In 1948, one-third of women were employed (the dashed line), and those women accounted for 28% of all employed persons (the dark gray line). The percent of women employed (the dashed line) peaked in 1999 at 60% and has been in decline since then. Women as a percent of all employed persons (the dark gray line) peaked in 2010 and has flatlined since then, but the number of women employed (the dotted line) continued its rise, interrupted only briefly during the Great Recession of 2008 to 2010.

Contrast the percent of women in the civilian labor force (the solid line in Figure 4.9)[25] with the percent of men in the civilian labor force (the dotted line), They seem to be on convergent paths that might even cross.

Figure 4.9: Annual U.S. Labor Force Participation Rates, 1948 – June 2022

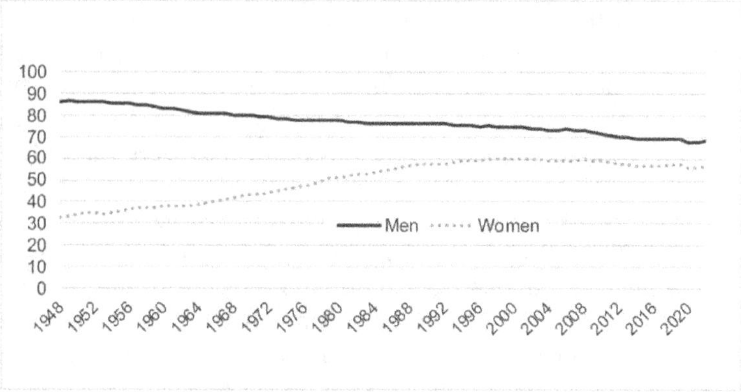

Source: U.S. Bureau of Labor Statistics

No definitive explanation exists for the decline of these labor force participation rates. For men, the decline can be attributed to rising income and the pension plans of major firms. In addition, the increased education periods for men compared to the conditions prior to World War II. For women, the same factors apply but do not seem in the aggregate to overcome the desirability of employment. American society changed after World War II. Home and vehicle ownership and the lower population

---

[25] The dashed grey line in Figure 4.8 and the black line in Figure 4.9 are not the same despite appearance. In Figure 4.8, we have the percent of employed women who are in the civilian non-institutional population (CNIP). In Figure 4.9, the numerator is different: It is the number of women in the labor force as a percent of the CNIP. The labor force includes both those employed and those unemployed. Figure 4.9 contains the Labor Force Participation Rates (LFPR) for males and females.

densities of suburbanization became more common. The larger refrigerator, the in-home washer and dryer, the vacuum cleaner, and a host of labor-saving products gave women more opportunities for education and marketable skills. The decline of women's labor force participation began when Baby Boomers started to turn fifty. At that point, 1996 and thereafter, the rise in participation rates plateaued and began a downward path similar to the men.

Labor force participation data come from Census Bureau household data, which do not have the certitude of submissions by employers to the Department of Labor concerning contributions to unemployment compensation funds. Three other factors might be contributing to the declines for both men and women noted in Figure 4.9. Large firms are shedding employees. Small proprietorships, partnerships, and gig workers are multiplying. Many of these firms involve few, if any, employees. Their principals may have a transitory or casual attachment to the labor market. Whereas the historical record shown in Figure 4.9 looks like a smooth progression, the most accurate conditions are best demonstrated by the annual change in the LFPRs of women and men (see Figure 4.10).

Between 1949 and 2022, women's LFPRs went up in 56 of 74 years, while the rates for men rose only 14 times in that span. The rates for men are clearly in decline throughout three-quarters of a century; the rates for women have been in a slow decline for one-quarter of a century (1996 to 2022). The most recent positive data for both sexes may be a short-term effect of the response to relaxations of Covid-19 policies.

Figure 4.10: Change in Annual U.S. Labor Force Participation Rates, 1949 – 2022

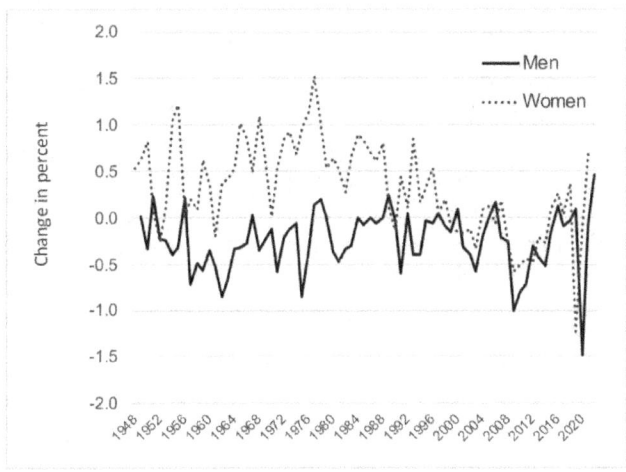

Source: U.S. Bureau of Labor Statistics

45

Women have been slowly gaining ground on men with regard to earnings from 1960 on. As shown in Table 4.2, women have averaged a 1.1% increase in median annual earnings compared to men's advance of 0.58% during those 61 years. This holds true for women of different races as well as the Hispanic/Non-Hispanic ethnic split. Over the longer period, Black women were the big winners, posting a 1.3% average annual gain with a $23,826 increase in earnings over the past 64 years. Hispanic men made the least progress in earnings, managing just $1,674 in total or a nebulous 0.08% per year.

In the Covid-19 crisis years (2019 to 2021), all groups shown in Table 4.2, except Black women, experienced earnings losses. The most severe in dollars and annual percent were Asian-American women and men. Did anti-Asian rhetoric, naming Covid "the China virus," have a hand in this discriminatory result?

Table 4.2: Median Earnings by Sex, Race, and Ethnicity

Long Term and Over the Covid Crisis

	Average Annual Percent Change	Dollar Gain Over Time	Years of Data	Covid Percent Loss	Covid Dollar Loss
Total Women	1.11%	25,078	1960 to 2021	-4.05%	-2,161
Total Men	0.58%	18,085	61 yrs	-4.73%	-3,037
White Women	0.98%	21,017	1967 to 2021	-4.28%	-2,298
White Men	0.30%	9,137	54 yrs	-4.67%	-3,024
Black Women	1.34%	23,826	1967 to 2021	2.86%	1,295
Black Men	0.73%	16,212	54 yrs	-5.05%	-2,667
Asian Women	1.23%	21,145	1988 to 2021	-10.94%	-7,842
Asian Men	0.95%	21,909	33 yrs	-5.25%	-4,534
Hispanic Women	0.63%	10,070	1974 to 2021	-2.56%	-1,039
Hispanic Men	0.08%	1,674	47 yrs	-2.82%	-1,329
White, non-Hispanic Women	1.00%	15,842	1987 to 2021	-1.83%	-1,034
White, non-Hispanic Men	0.32%	7,065	34 yrs	-1.91%	-1,349

Constant 2021 dollars

Source: U.S. Bureau of Labor Statistics

Women's share of both earnings and employment for the decade 2011 to 2021 indicate that neither changed much over time. (Figure 4.11)

Figure 4.11: Full-Time U.S. Wage and Salaried Workers, 2011 – 2021

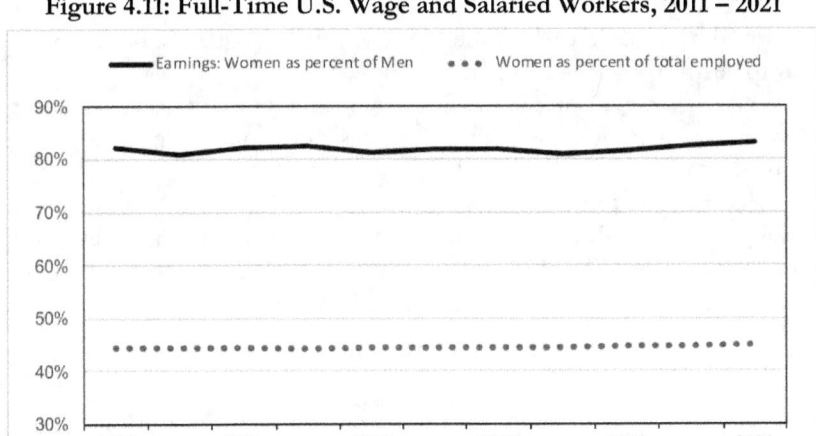

Source: U.S. Bureau of Labor Statistics

A more detailed examination of the earnings data for different age groups in Figure 4.12 shows that the relationship between the sexes, although variable, demonstrated little progress or regression.

Figure 4.12: Full-Time Wage and Salary Workers' Weekly Median Earnings

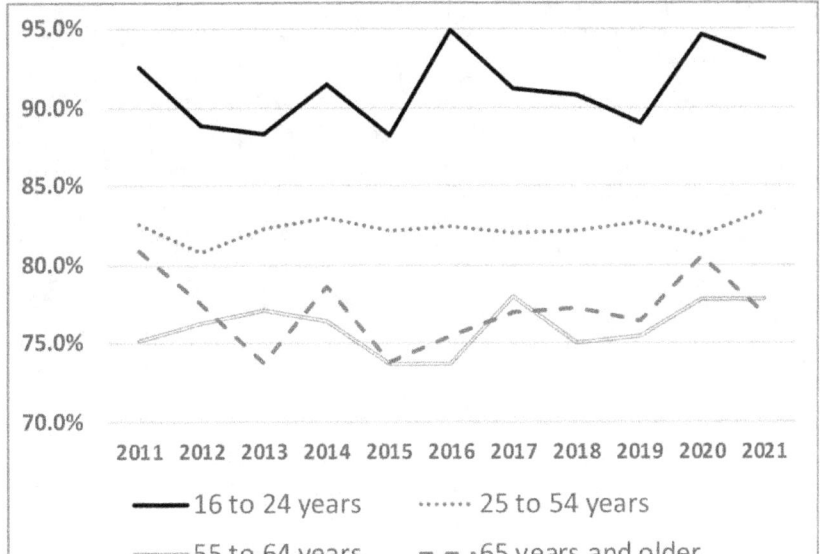

Source: U.S. Bureau of Labor Statistics

Underlying these results is the simple fact that women as a percent of employed persons, in each of the four identified age groups, hardly varied year to year throughout this period. [26]

While these aggregates show little progress in the earnings gap between men and women, perhaps such differences can be found in the available occupational, racial, and ethnic data.

One of the underlying reasons given for the discrepancies between the earnings of men and women is that women are, or have been, denied entry into many occupations. This discrimination might be on the basis of education, training, or location, in line with cultural bias.

Occupations

What one earns is a function of the occupation s/he enters. In 1920, the top occupation for women was domestic and personal services, aside from separately identified positions such as cooks and laundresses (Table 4.3). From 1930 to 1950, the top occupation was manufacturing work. Thereafter, white collar jobs became the leading occupations for women.

Table 4.3: Top Occupations of Women since 1920

Year	Share of Women Employed in Top 10 Occupations	Top Occupations of Employed Women	Number of Employed Women in the Occupation	Percent of Employed Women in the Occupation	Percent of All Women in Labor Force
1920	52.80%	Other Domestic and Personal Service	669,491	15.50%	8.20%
1930	66.20%	Operatives (n.e.c.)	1,386,515	19.90%	13.20%
1940	67.90%	Operatives (n.e.c.)	1,848,824	21.30%	14.40%
1950	69.80%	Operatives (n.e.c.)	2,461,939	21.20%	14.80%
1960	56.10%	Clerks (n.e.c.)	1,725,420	13.80%	7.80%
1970	42.10%	Secretaries	2,625,600	20.30%	8.60%
1980	41.10%	Secretaries	3,820,700	20.80%	8.60%
1990	36.30%	Secretaries	3,823,250	18.60%	6.80%
2000	33.60%	Secretaries and Administrative Assistants	3,597,416	16.60%	5.60%
2010	33.30%	Teachers	3,984,836	16.10%	5.40%
2019	32.20%	Teachers	4,364,262	17.10%	5.50%

(n.e.c.) = Not elsewhere classified

Source: Women's Bureau, U.S. Department of Labor

---

[26] The greatest deviation was a mere -0.13% among those 25-54 years of age, with correspondingly small positive deviations in the other age groups.

Both Figure 4.13 below and Table 4.3 demonstrate the broadening of occupations open to women as a result of greater educational opportunity and its collateral benefit—certificates of completion. In the early years, more than two-thirds of all women worked in the top ten occupations. By 2019, less than one-third were in the top ten. Further, as Figure 4.13 indicates, the widening gap between the index of labor force participation (the dashed line) and that of holding a top-ten job (the dotted line) similarly suggests job diversification.

Figure 4.13: Women in the Labor Force and in Top Ten Occupations

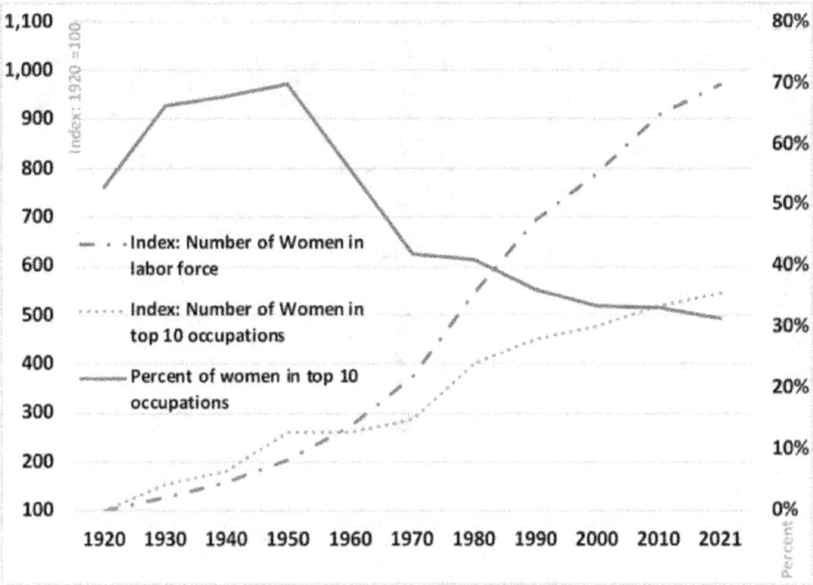

Source: U.S. Bureau of Labor Statistics

Specifically, as occupations diversified and acquired increasing complexity, the top ten went from involving 53% of employed women to 31% as shown in Figure 4.13 above and Table 4.4 below. By 2021, in only a few occupations did women exceed or match men in both number of jobs and level of remuneration. Of 152 occupations, we found eight where both conditions were met (see Table 4.4).

Table 4.4: Top ten Occupations of Women in 1920 and 2019

Top 10 Occupations of Employed Women, 1920	Number of Employed Women in the Occupation	Share of Women Employed in Top 10 Occupations	Top 10 Occupations of Employed Women, 2019	Number of Employed Women in the Occupation	Share of Women Employed in Top 10 Occupations
Other Domestic and Personal Service	669,491	8.19%	Teachers	4,364,262	5.49%
Teachers	622,877	7.62%	Nurses	3,808,657	4.79%
Stenographers and Typewriters	567,784	6.94%	Nursing, Psychiatric, and Home Health Aides	3,058,071	3.85%
Clerks (n.e.c.)	442,753	5.41%	Secretaries and Administrative Assistants	2,618,644	3.30%
Farm Laborers, Home Farm	396,625	4.85%	Cashiers	2,362,581	2.97%
Launderers and Laundresses	384,083	4.70%	Customer Service Representatives	1,909,145	2.40%
Salesmen and Saleswomen, Stores	350,552	4.29%	Retail Salespersons	1,658,665	2.09%
Bookkeepers and Cashiers	337,418	4.13%	Managers, n.e.c.	1,627,361	2.05%
Cooks	266,801	3.26%	Waiters and Waitresses	1,515,247	1.91%
Farmers, General Farms	240,385	2.94%	First-Line Supervisors of Retail Sales Workers	1,464,164	1.84%
Total	4,278,769	53.30%	Total	24,386,797	30.70%

Source: U.S. Bureau of Labor Statistics

As compliance officers, women exceeded the annual average weekly earnings of full-time men by 6.4%. But as teaching assistants, where women exceeded the number of men by nearly 400%, their earnings superiority was a mere 0.3%. Female pharmacists are found nearly 19% more frequently than their male counterparts, and earn only 4% more than them. But most commonly, women do not have parity with men in earnings for the same occupation. Of 152 occupations in 2021, women who were chief executives were 43% of men in numbers, but make only 70% of men in earnings. First-line women supervisors are only 23% of men in numbers holding such jobs, and also 70% in terms of earnings.

Table 4.5: Women's Full-Time Jobs and Earnings, 2021

	Women		Women as a Percent of Men		
	Number of Workers (000)	Median Weekly Earnings ($)	Number of Workers	Median Weekly Earnings	Rank in 152
Top Ten Occupations by Earnings Parity					
Compliance Officers	137	1,423	100.00%	106.90%	1
Graphic Designers	91	1,225	102.20%	106.40%	2
Clinical Laboratory Technologists and Technicians	210	1,001	187.50%	103.80%	3
Pharmacists	133	2,087	118.80%	103.80%	4
Insurance Claims and Policy Processing Clerks	202	766	336.70%	101.60%	5
Billing and Posting Clerks	346	774	652.80%	100.90%	6
Teaching Assistants	687	641	592.20%	100.30%	7
Purchasing Agents, Except Wholesale, Retail, and Farm Products	132	1,165	165.00%	100.00%	8
Cashiers	888	513	256.60%	98.70%	9
Fast Food and Counter Workers	172	503	179.20%	98.40%	10
Bottom Ten Occupations by Earnings Parity					
Chief Executives	348	1,904	43.30%	70.00%	143
First-Line Supervisors of Production and Operating Workers	137	796	22.80%	69.90%	144
Sales and Related Occupations	4,191	720	82.30%	68.60%	145
Medical Assistants	430	668	843.10%	68.20%	146
Insurance Sales Agents	249	839	116.90%	67.00%	147
Other Engineering Technologists and Technicians, Except Drafters	52	903	23.40%	66.10%	148
Personal Financial Advisors	154	1,424	65.50%	65.20%	149
Medical Scientists	59	1,368	103.50%	59.70%	150
Legal Occupations	807	1,332	135.90%	59.70%	151
Securities, Commodities, and Financial Services Sales Agents	69	1,054	50.40%	55.70%	152

Source: Census Bureau, Current Population Survey, 2021 (Table 39)

Occupations are subsets of industries. Under "construction" there are plumbers, carpenters, and electricians. Healthcare includes too many subsets for the mind to comprehend. One may choose an occupation, but s/he often has little choice of the industry employing that role. The more skilled or knowledgeable a person might be, the more narrow the range of attainable industries. Cardiologists are rarely found on construction sites; similarly, plumbers generally don't perform open-heart surgeries.

Cultural factors over time play a role in choices made with regard to occupations and industries. When we find only a small percent of women engaged in construction (1.6% of all women compared to 12.2% of men), are we surprised? Is it discrimination by contractors and unions rather than preconceptions by women that yields the gender dominance rankings in Table 4.6?

Table 4.6: Industry and Gender Percentages, 2019

	In Descending Order of Male Dominance		
	Percent Distribution Among Industries		
	Women	Men	Difference
Total Employed Persons, 16 Years and Older	100	100	Men - Women
Construction	1.6	12.2	10.6
Durable Goods Manufacturing	3.4	8.9	5.5
Transportation and Warehousing	2.6	6.9	4.3
Wholesale Trade	1.4	3	1.6
Nondurable Goods Manufacturing	2.9	4.4	1.5
Professional and Technical Services	7.4	8.8	1.4
Management, Administrative, and Waste Services	3.6	5	1.4
Agriculture, Forestry, Fishing, and Hunting	0.9	2.1	1.2
Utilities	0.4	1.3	0.9
Mining, Quarrying, and Oil and Gas Extraction	0.2	0.8	0.6
Information	1.5	2	0.5
Public Administration	4.5	4.7	0.2
Arts, Entertainment, and Recreation	2.1	2.2	0.1
Real Estate and Rental and Leasing	2.1	2.1	0
Retail Trade	10.4	10.2	-0.2
Other Services, Except Private Households	4.5	4.1	-0.4
Other Services	1	0.1	-0.9
Finance and Insurance	5.5	4.1	-1.4
Accommodation and Food Services	8	6.3	-1.7
Social Assistance	3.9	0.7	-3.2
Hospitals	7.5	2.2	-5.3
Educational Services	13.3	5.2	-8.1
Health Services, Except Hospitals	11.5	2.8	-8.7

Source: U.S. Bureau of Labor Statistics

For women and men to have the same industry profile, where the percent of each gender was identical in each industry, as in the case of real estate, nearly 30% of those at work would have to be put in motion, changing industries until all the differences above were zero. That said, we expect differences in the employment of women according to occupation and industry. Should those differences persist from place to place? What happens when we hold occupation constant? In Table 4.7 women's earnings in five regionally diverse states are examined. The occupations chosen were accountants and auditors, a professional activity, somewhat regulated with an expectation of specialized training and education.

Table 4.7: Women's Median Earnings in Five States

Accountants and Auditors, All Women					
	Alabama	**Indiana**	**New Jersey**	**Oklahoma**	**Oregon**
Median Earnings	53,813	53,692	71,436	52,935	56,613
Percent of Men's Earnings	75.40%	74.30%	77.60%	74.80%	73.00%
Percent of Women in Occupation	65.40%	61.00%	50.30%	63.60%	66.60%

Women's Median earnings as percent of Men's earnings by Race / Ethnicity					
White Alone	72.10%	72.20%	75.20%	69.90%	71.30%
Black or African American Alone	94.30%	104.70%	85.70%	110.30%	110.10%
Asian Alone	79.30%	103.30%	77.70%	102.00%	76.50%
Hispanic or Latino	218.70%	65.80%	87.70%	94.60%	99.40%
Balance of Not Hispanic or Latino	74.90%	64.40%	63.10%	95.10%	88.20%
American Indian and Alaska Native Alone				78.60%	104.90%

Women's Median Earnings by Race / Ethnicity as Percent of All Women's Earnings					
White Alone	99.70%	100.60%	103.90%	102.00%	100.40%
Black or African American Alone	101.00%	96.40%	87.80%	88.60%	143.40%
Asian Alone	92.60%	123.00%	102.60%	90.70%	99.40%
Hispanic or Latino	111.80%	74.40%	86.20%	87.80%	81.30%
Balance of Not Hispanic or Latino	98.60%	98.90%	89.10%	108.40%	95.80%
American Indian and Alaska Native Alone				96.50%	98.40%

Source: U.S. Bureau of Labor Statistics

The median annual earnings of accounting and auditing women in four of the five states have a narrow range of $3,678, with a spread of only 6.8% from the low of Oklahoma's $53,935 to Oregon's $56,613. But New Jersey's $71,436 shows significantly higher earnings. Despite this bonanza, New Jersey's female accountants and auditors earn just 77.6% of men's earnings, which is similar to the gender differential in the other four states. Women in accounting and auditing occupy over 60% of all such jobs, except in New Jersey where the figure is just over 50%. Yet one doesn't identify this profession as predominantly female and not one where the earnings of women would be below that of women in other economic roles.

Further examination of Table 4.7 reveals that white women in each of the five states have a lower percent of earnings compared to the total of all women in that state. Black women generally do better than Black men across all states, such as in Indiana, Oklahoma, and Oregon. Only in New Jersey, regardless of race, are women in the profession failing to match or exceed the earnings of males.

With Whites likely to dominate the number of women accountants and auditors in most states, the median for all women in a state will be close to the median for Whites only. The positive outliers (10% higher than men) are Blacks in Oregon, Asians in Indiana, and Hispanics in Alabama. Of the negative outliers, Indiana's Hispanic women stand alone, 25% below the figure for all women.

Career Paths

Part of the wage gap seen thus far is also related to the status that women hold within a given occupation or industry. Women may become fully certified accountants and auditors, but what progress do they make on the career ladder? Compensation often depends not only on such factors as seniority but on the number of employees and functions as well as the span of control exercised by the individual.

In Figure 4.14, data are presented for men and women in three age groups and four status levels. The most telling observation shows that men advance in status as they age, whereas women show little change in status in their mature years.

Figure 4.14: Career Progression by Sex and Age

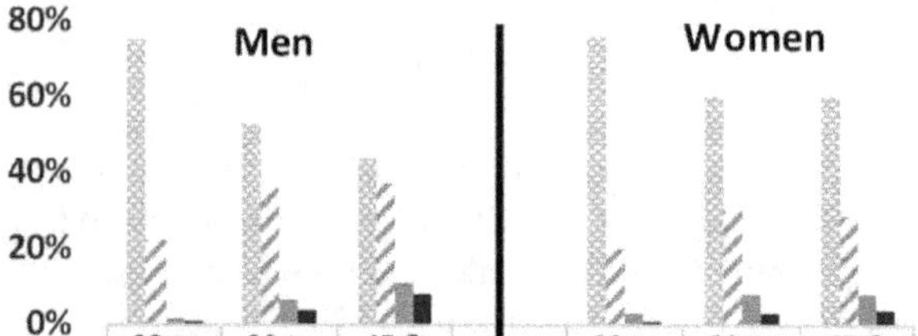

	Men			Women		
	20 to 29	30 to 44	45 & older	20 to 29	30 to 44	45 & older
Individual contributor	75%	53%	44%	76%	60%	60%
Manager/ Supervisor	22%	36%	37%	20%	30%	29%
Director	2%	7%	11%	3%	8%	8%
Executive	1%	4%	8%	1%	3%	4%

Source: U.S. Bureau of Labor Statistics

In the youngest group, ages 20 to 29, the differences in status are small. To achieve parity in status would require a movement of only 2% of the employees. Parity at ages 30 to 44 requires a movement of 8%; the figure is doubled to 16% at ages 45 and older. These may be the residuals of prior gender discrimination or career differentiation. For example, men may be more willing to move geographically in order to accept a more responsible position. We may find that differences in status, according to age and sex, will decline in the future. Being a woman may be the most crucial factor in suppressing earnings, but it is not the only characteristic of note. Race, ethnicity, and location play positive or negative roles in specific circumstances.

Living arrangements

Households are economic units more significant than any individual person; they are the actors making decisions about spending and working. Refrigerators and washing machines are sold to households. The capacities and features of those appliances may vary with the number and nature of the inhabitants, but few households have more than one. As incomes have risen and technology has advanced, the number of radios, TVs, and telephones have trended faster than the number of people. Many a person living alone will have more than one TV but only one waffle iron.

How Americans arrange themselves in households has changed over the years. The familiar four-person unit of Mom, Dad, and the kids has been transformed into several variants. In 2021, data from the Census Bureau indicated that adult women live in 70% of America's 127.5 million households, as shown in Table 4.8 below, where seven different household types are identified. Most prevalent are the 59.6 million opposite-sex married couples, constituting two- thirds of all households with adult females. They are joined by 8.7 million opposite-sex cohabiting couples to comprise nearly 77% of all households with resident adult females. The next largest group of households are those with females living alone, 19.7 million or 22% of the households in Table 4.8. Of women who live solo, 12 million are under age 65 and 7.7 million are 65 or older. [27]

---

[27] When 16.4 million males living alone are added to this group, they comprise 28.7% of all U.S. households and 11% of all persons. These numbers are increasingly recognized by advertisers.

Table 4.8 Households with Female Residents

	Living Circumstances					
	Opposite-Sex	Same-Sex	Living Alone	Unrelated	Totals	Percent
Totals	68,345,629	631,873	19,691,382	549,682	89,218,566	100%
Percent	76.60%	0.70%	22.10%	0.60%	100%	
Couples with Females Partners						
Married	59,648,955	374,207			60,023,162	67.30%
Cohabiting	8,696,674	257,666			8,954,340	10.00%
Under Age 65			12,013,257		12,013,257	13.50%
65 and Older			7,678,125		7,678,125	8.60%
Living with Another Person				549,682	549,682	0.60%

Source: Calculated from Census Bureau American Community Survey, 2021

How do households differ in spending? Figure 4.15 offers some answers for the period 1984 to 2020. Not all household types are represented because some were not separately enumerated in previous years.

Figure 4.15: Relative Expenditures of U.S. Households, 1984 – 2020

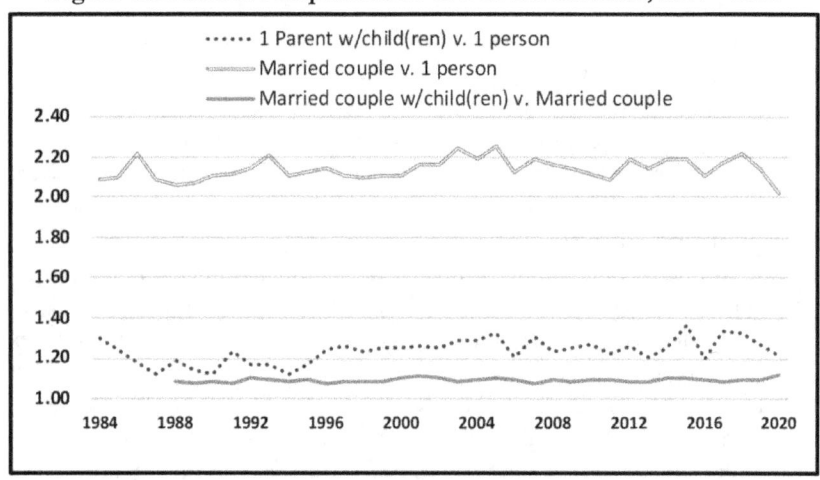

Source: Bureau of Labor Statistics, Consumer Expenditure Surveys

Can two live as cheaply as one? Possibly, but without further detailed analysis of age and other factors, the tentative answer is "That's not how they do live." A married couple, over the course of 38 recent years, spent more than twice the amount of a single person.[28] The lowest differential was in the first year of the Covid-19 pandemic, 2020.

---

[28] The average differential is 14% above twice the expenditures of a single person. The range of the data points is 11% of the median differential.

A child or children appear to increase the expenditures of a single parent by 24%. Once again, other factors such as income need to be considered. Yet we must wonder if the support given by governments to low-income single parents adequately compensates for this differential.[29] The expenditures of married couples with children averaged 9% more than those of married couples without children.[30] Older couples whose children no longer live in the household may have higher expenditures levels associated with higher living levels than younger couples with resident children. Hence the 9% differential may not accurately reflect variation in the story.

Because these data are so readily available, they are likely to be widely used by writers, advocates, and propagandists who thrive on low-cost data. It is easy to then build policies and programs when there is a sense of urgency and no tolerance for complexity. Such practices also lead to underfunding the collection and analysis of data which might lead to more sensible and effective action.

Domestic production, the use of time, and GDP

As discussed above, the U.S. Bureau of Economic Analysis (BEA) has developed a separate, fledgling account for domestic production which can be added to existing market estimates for GDP. It is predicated on the American Time Use Survey (ATUS) from the Bureau of Labor Statistics (BLS) and collected by the Census Bureau. Such cooperation is both commendable and understandable for its circular deniability characteristic of large organizations.

What is domestic production? BEA uses the following activities to define our at-home activities:
- cooking
- housework
- odd jobs
- gardening
- shopping
- childcare
- domestic travel to facilitate the functions above

---

[29] The range of these data over the median is 20%, or nearly double that of the previously discussed differential.

[30] The range of these data over the median is a mere 4% and consistent with the very flat line shown.

Given these seven categories, how many hours per week do people spend in domestic production? Figure 4.16 (BEA's numbering) provides answers for men and women, employed and not employed.[31] It is evident that regardless of employment status, women spend a great deal more time in domestic production than men. That difference appears to be steady over time by ten hours per week. In each case, the amount of time spent in domestic production is on a slow path downwards. For each of the functions above, a chart is provided in the Data Appendix. How do these time allocations translate into GDP? BEA's methodology seeks the market price to hire someone to engage in these activities.

Figure 4.16: Total Weekly Hours by Demographic Group, 2003 – 2020

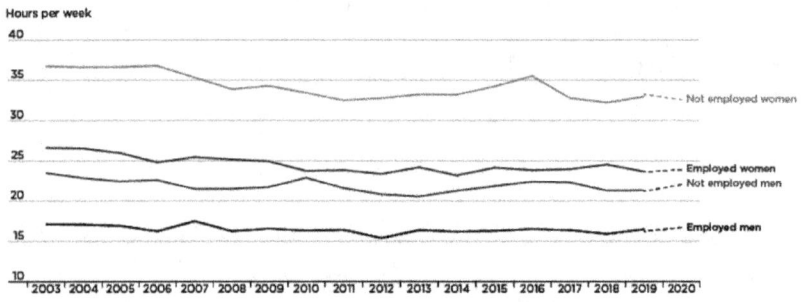

Source: U.S. Bureau of Economic Analysis

In addition, BEA calculates a depreciation or use factor for each capital asset employed in domestic production. The washing machine and microwave have costs in whatever activity they partake. We may not consider such factors as we rummage in the refrigerator during the wee hours of the morning, but such calculations are appropriate if we seek to place domestic production on a par with market, not-for-profit, and government production.

BEA estimates domestic production in 2020 was valued at $5.3 trillion or 19.% of GDP. To put that number in perspective, let's consider the equation:

Y= C+I+G or Income = Consumption + Investment + Government Spending

---

[31] Data for 2020 were estimated, given prior BLS weights, because of Covid data collection interruptions.

In 2020, private sector investment equaled $2.7 trillion (10.5% of GDP), and government spending equaled $3.9 trillion (14.7% of GDP). From Figure 4.16 above, we find that women accounted for 57 hours (58.8%) of the 97 total hours per week devoted to domestic production. If we assume that the hours of work by men and by women are equal in value (arguably a flawed idea), we would have women providing $3.1 trillion in domestic production, 11.9% of GDP.

Consumer expenditures

Has the increased presence of women in the workforce changed the relative importance of various goods and services? The answer is YES, but the point is difficult to prove. We can agree that more families eat out today than at the end of World War I. But 21st-century Americans have more income and live in more densely populated areas than a hundred years ago. Cooking is seldom taught in high schools these days. Family recipe books, while still highly valued, are less frequently found on household bookshelves.

Clothing styles have changed for men and women. Vulgarity in speech has increased. Popular music is dominated by raucous sound at ear-popping volume. Automobile ownership and use have multiplied. The square footage of homes has increased dramatically. Can anyone support the idea that these are exclusively, or even mainly, the result of increased participation by women in the economy?

Women's liberation, by whatever name one chooses, has been a positive force in our economy. But little has been proven about the extent of benefits compared to whatever costs may have been incurred. Nonetheless, there remain limitations on women's full participation in economic affairs that will be tested and removed as 18th-century Enlightenment ideas are played out.

Chapter Five: The Change of Life

Sheila Kennedy

The phrase "change of life" is usually shorthand for female menopause. In this chapter, however, we use that phrase to refer to the philosophical, legal, and cultural changes that have gradually transformed women's lives. Those changes have been greatly facilitated by the ability to control reproduction, discussed in Chapter Two, and by the labor-saving devices discussed in Chapters Three and Four, but they have also benefited from what we might call an "iterative relationship" with the feminist thought and political activism that have changed American law and culture.

Feminism Then and Now

The seeds of today's feminism were planted during the Enlightenment, as women began to argue that emerging perspectives on liberty and natural rights should apply to both men and women. Few of the leading philosophers of the day agreed. Rousseau, for example, considered women silly creatures, clearly subordinate to men.[32] Important documents of the time, arguing for natural rights, rarely addressed the legal status of women. An exception was Mary Wollstonecraft's pivotal *Vindication of the Rights of Woman*. Published in 1792, it made the case that women and men should be given equal opportunities in education, work, and politics. Wollstonecraft argued that, if women were indeed "silly," it was due to a society that trained them to be that way.

In the United States, what is usually considered the "first wave" of feminism found expression in the movement for woman suffrage, which was finally achieved in 1920 with the ratification of the Nineteenth Amendment to the Constitution. The 1800s had been a mixed bag for women's rights. There was some progress: as early as 1839, Mississippi granted women the right to own property in their own name, and in 1869, Arabella Mansfield was admitted to the bar in Iowa, making her the first woman lawyer in the country. In 1872, Victoria Woodhull, nominated by the National Radical Reformers (a breakaway faction of the National Woman Suffrage Association), became the first woman to run for President. In 1887, the town of Argonia, Kansas, elected a woman mayor,

---

[32] "Rousseau's Take on Women and Education" https://www.thoughtco.com/rousseau-on-women-and-education-3528799_[accessed 9/2/22]

and in 1890, Wyoming became the first state to give women the right to vote.

In contrast to those victories, the same year that Woodhull ran for President, Susan B. Anthony tried to cast a ballot in her hometown of Rochester, New York; she was testing whether the language of the Fourteenth Amendment would be interpreted broadly enough to allow women to vote. It wasn't, and she was convicted of the crime of unlawful voting. In 1873, the Supreme Court confirmed the right of states to exclude married women from the practice of law.

That "first wave" of feminist activity subsided after passage of the Nineteenth Amendment, but nevertheless the early 1900s were years of additional progress. By 1900, every state allowed women to own property, and in 1916, Jeannette Rankin became the first woman elected to the U.S. House of Representatives. Margaret Sanger won a lawsuit allowing doctors to discuss birth control (for health reasons only!) with their married patients, and Frances Perkins became the first woman to serve in the President's Cabinet in 1933. But it wasn't until the latter half of the twentieth century, with the emergence of the so-called "second wave" of feminism, that a steady stream of legislation securing women's rights began to eliminate the legal barriers that continued to keep women second-class citizens. (We will discuss the most significant of those legislative victories—and defeats—in the second part of this chapter.)

What is now known as "second wave" feminism began in the wake of World War II and blossomed in the 1960s and '70s. Much of that feminist activism was triggered by the publication of Betty Friedan's 1963 book, *The Feminine Mystique*. The book was a best-seller, widely read and discussed; it cataloged the symptoms of what Friedan dubbed "the problem that has no name," and charged that the era's culturally celebrated suburban domesticity was boring and suffocating, especially for women who had emerged with degrees from the colleges and universities that were now open to them. In the wake of its publication, thousands of women established "consciousness-raising" groups in which they read feminist tracts and discussed the numerous legal inequities and cultural attitudes that prevented their full participation in the economic and political life of the country.

Historians suggest that first-wave feminists had been inspired by the abolition movement's rhetoric of equality and that their great-granddaughters drew inspiration from the rhetoric of the civil rights movement and protests against the Vietnam War.

Unlike first-wave feminism that had subsumed a variety of philosophical disagreements under the overarching goal of securing the vote, second-wave feminism was more fragmented, with contending arguments about both feminist theory and political strategy. As the Encyclopedia Britannica reports on the period, the second wave

> provoked extensive theoretical discussion about the origins of women's oppression, the nature of gender, and the role of the family. Kate Millett's Sexual Politics made the best-seller list in 1970, and in it she broadened the term politics to include all "power-structured relationships" and posited that the personal was actually political. Shulamith Firestone, a founder of the New York Radical Feminists, published The Dialectic of Sex in the same year, insisting that love disadvantaged women by creating intimate shackles between them and the men they loved—men who were also their oppressors. One year later, Germaine Greer, an Australian living in London, published The Female Eunuch, in which she argued that the sexual repression of women cuts them off from the creative energy they need to be independent and self-fulfilled.

> Any attempt to create a coherent, all-encompassing feminist ideology was doomed. While most could agree on the questions that needed to be asked about the origins of gender distinctions, the nature of power, or the roots of sexual violence, the answers to those questions were bogged down by ideological hairsplitting, name-calling, and mutual recrimination. Even the term liberation could mean different things to different people. Feminism became a river of competing eddies and currents.[33]

As we will see shortly, those "eddies and currents," discordant though they often were, led to activism that produced a substantial expansion of women's legal rights. Although it is not the focus of this investigation, it's important to note that many feminists have also been prominent advocates for the rights of other marginalized groups, and especially for Black women. It is equally important to acknowledge that feminist anti-racism came late to a movement historically dominated by White middle-class women and that large numbers of those women had for many years been oblivious to the precarity and oppression of their Black sisters.

---

[33] "The second wave of feminism" https://www.britannica.com/topic/feminism/The-second-wave-of-feminism [accessed on 9/3/22]

The third wave (or fourth—there isn't even current agreement among activists on whether today's feminism should be considered third or fourth wave) was given impetus by the fact that women have finally achieved substantial economic and professional power, although the extent of that power and the degree to which equity has been achieved remain matters of intense debate. The arguments around and within feminism—what the term actually means, the differences between equality and equity, liberation and parity, what the movement should mean for questions of sexual behavior, sexual orientation, and gender identity, and differences in the status and prospects of Black and White women—now reach a far broader audience, thanks to social media and the internet.

Until the Supreme Court's decision in *Dobbs*, the third (or fourth) wave was largely, albeit not exclusively, a movement of scholars and activists who, among many other things, have been redefining sexual liberation to include issues of racism, sexual orientation, and gender fluidity. The movement is also grappling with intersectionality, a term coined in 1989 by Kimberlé Crenshaw, a law professor and social theorist. Intersectionality recognizes that people are often disadvantaged by multiple sources of marginalization: their race, class, gender identity, sexual orientation, religion, and other identity markers. Intersectionality recognizes that those identity markers—for example, "woman" and "Black"—don't exist independently of each other. That is, in the lives of real people, each identity informs and affects the others. The complex and often contradictory scholarship of feminism has given birth to multiple approaches to activism and spawned a number of factions: among them are liberal feminism, materialist-Socialist feminism, radical feminism, psychoanalytic feminism, and womanist feminism. Despite their differences in emphases and strategies (some of which can seem politically tone-deaf), the various philosophical strands have each arguably contributed to slow but steady progress for women. Feminist arguments have made society more equal for women and have dismantled many of the legal and cultural barriers that have operated to disadvantage women.

Politics and the Law

A visual timeline of women's political participation would show a steady upward climb. In 1932, the first woman elected to the U.S. Senate was Arkansas' Hattie Wyatt Caraway, who has largely been neglected by history. For three more decades, little else relevant to women's legal progress occurred. But in 1963, with the passage of the Equal Pay Act, Congress required equal pay for equal work, irrespective of the race, religion, national origin, or gender of the worker. The Equal Pay Act was followed by Title VII of the Civil Rights Act of 1964. Title VII prohibited sex discrimination in employment, and created the Equal Employment Opportunity Commission (EEOC). Political scuttlebutt claims that women were included in the Civil Rights Act—which was primarily intended to outlaw discrimination on the basis of race—as a last-ditch effort to derail its passage. Southern lawmakers opposed to the bill thought that the addition of protections for women would surely kill it.

In 1965, the Supreme Court handed down the landmark case of *Griswold v. Connecticut*. In that case, the court ruled that the state of Connecticut lacked the authority to prohibit married couples from using contraception. The court based its decision on a determination that the Bill of Rights, properly understood, protects a zone of individual privacy. The case established the doctrine of substantive due process—basically, the rule that government must respect the right of individuals to determine certain private or "intimate" matters for themselves; it drew a line between decisions that government could properly control and those that were to be left to individuals' self-determination.

Women won additional rights during the 1960s and '70s. In 1968, President Johnson issued an executive order prohibiting sex discrimination by government contractors, and requiring that affirmative action plans include women. In 1969, California passed the nation's first "no-fault" divorce law. In 1972, Title IX prohibited sex discrimination in education programs receiving federal funding, and in 1973, the Supreme Court handed down its decision in *Roe v. Wade*, affirming a pregnant woman's right to terminate a pregnancy.

In 1974, Congress outlawed housing and credit discrimination against women, and the Court ruled that businesses couldn't require pregnant women to take leaves of absence—that the need for such leaves is properly determined on a case-by-case basis. It was 1975 before the Supreme Court denied states the right to exclude women from juries and 1978 before Congress passed an act banning discrimination against pregnant women.

The legal landscape after 1978 has been a mixture of hits and misses. As recently as 1981, the Supreme Court ruled that it is constitutional to exclude women from the draft. That year, however, the court did strike down state laws that had designated husbands "heads and masters" of a married household and that gave those "masters" sole control of joint property. The court went on to ban sex discrimination in previously all-male service organizations like Kiwanis in 1984 and affirmed that hostile and/or abusive workplaces were a form of discrimination on the basis of sex in 1986. But in 1989, the court ruled that states could deny public funding for abortions and could pass laws prohibiting public hospitals from performing them. In 2000, a mere six years after its passage, the court invalidated portions of the Violence Against Women Act, which has lapsed, and at this writing has not been reauthorized.

In one of the earliest indications of hostility to women's right to terminate a pregnancy, Congress passed the pejoratively titled "Partial Birth Abortion Ban Act" in 2005 and a year later, the court upheld it. "Partial Birth Abortion" was the label used by abortion opponents to suggest that late-term abortions were really a form of infanticide, rather than the extremely rare and tragic situations that prompt such late-term terminations—usually, a fetal abnormality inconsistent with life or a threat to the life of the mother.

Despite some legislative victories during the early 2000s, passage of the Lilly Ledbetter Fair Pay Restoration Act in 2009 and removal of the ban forbidding women from serving in the military in 2013, the growing resistance to women's rights was gathering momentum, thanks to its embrace by the GOP. In 2012, the Paycheck Fairness Act failed in the Senate on a party-line vote, and state-level restrictions on reproductive choice supported by Republicans multiplied. Those attacks were not limited to abortion access; several Supreme Court decisions made access to birth control more difficult. One of the most egregious was the court's ruling in *Burwell v. Hobby Lobby Stores*, a case that deserves special attention because it was a harbinger of what would follow.

Hobby Lobby is a closely held corporation and a national retailer of craft supplies. The company sued the federal government over a provision in the Affordable Care Act (ACA), requiring businesses that provide employees with health insurance to include birth control as one of the benefits of that coverage. The owners/shareholders of the corporation claimed that the requirement (which, thanks to other provisions of the ACA, cost them nothing) violated their First Amendment free exercise rights—rights that had never previously been asserted by or accorded to a corporation.

In a 5-4 decision authored by Justice Samuel Alito, the court ruled in their favor. Had Hobby Lobby been a sole proprietorship or partnership, the court's ruling would have fallen within existing First Amendment jurisprudence. But Hobby Lobby—"closely held" or not—is a for-profit corporation and the decision was a jarring departure from prior jurisprudence. Critics pointed out that when people choose to do business using the corporate form, the law grants them certain benefits that are unavailable to unincorporated individuals. Most significantly, they are shielded from personal liability. That is, if someone sues Hobby Lobby and wins a huge judgment, they can recover from whatever assets the corporation owns, but they cannot "pierce the corporate veil" and take the owners' personal assets. That protection against personal liability is the main reason for the legal fiction we call a corporation, and it is meant to encourage people to go into business. In effect, the government says to potential entrepreneurs, "If you'll engage in economic activity, we'll protect you from a significant measure of risk. You may lose the business, but you won't lose your house."

The owners of Hobby Lobby wanted the benefits of the corporate form but not the obligations. Their argument was essentially that a rule they didn't like shouldn't apply to a company with "sincerely" religious shareholders. Tellingly, they asked the court to pierce the corporate veil and treat the company as a sole proprietorship *for this purpose only*. At one point, the majority opinion explicitly noted that the company wanted to act in accordance with its owners' religion without losing the benefits of the corporate form. Justice Alito's decision allowed the owner/shareholders to use their religion—"sincerely-held" or not—to impose an additional cost on female employees whose own personal and religious beliefs allowed them to use contraception.

Once Amy Coney Barrett was named to the court to augment the path of Justice Alito and the four justices who had joined him in the *Hobby Lobby* decision, the further implications of that case became clear. The court majority that handed down *Dobbs* departed significantly from precedents that have shaped American law and culture for fifty years. Those precedents had empowered women and changed the culture. In 2022, the overriding political question was whether *Hobby Lobby*, *Dobbs* and other cases privileging conservative Christian beliefs, together with the frantic opposition of Christian Nationalists to non-male, non-white, non-Christian Americans would be sufficient to reverse the hard-won gains of previously marginalized Americans, very much including female Americans.

The Culture

The technological and legal changes that have permitted women to participate far more fully in the labor force and in political life have had a significant effect upon the American cultural landscape. As this is written, there are 24 women serving in the U.S. Senate and 122 in the House. (Granted, that's not parity; it represents 24% in the Senate and 28% in the House.) A woman is currently the Vice-President of the United States, and a woman—Hillary Clinton—won the popular vote for President by some three million votes in 2016. Women are ambassadors, heads of agencies, and Cabinet members. Currently, there are nine women serving as governors of their states and in 2023 there will be twelve. Americans have become used to seeing, and voting for, female candidates for state legislative positions. Females may not yet have achieved parity, but most of the American public has become accustomed to their political presence.

Political participation is an important element of the change in women's status but hardly the only one. When we turn to economic participation, we find that more than 11.6 million firms are owned by women; those firms employ nearly nine million people and generated $1.7 trillion in sales as of 2017.[34] Female athletes have made significant inroads into sports that have long been seen as male-dominated, and thanks to their recent activism, there has been substantial movement toward pay equity. When Americans turn on their televisions, they see women news anchors and sports reporters; when young people enroll in institutions of higher learning, increasing numbers of their professors are women, and 47% of those institutions currently have women presidents.[35] Contemporary Americans are accustomed to seeing women perform as astronauts, CEOs, soldiers, doctors, and lawyers. Today's America looks dramatically different from the America into which the country's older citizens were born.

That said, it remains true that women have less personal autonomy, fewer resources at their disposal, and more limited influence over the decision-making processes that shape today's society. Polling suggests that most Americans recognize that there is more work to do, and want that progress to continue, but survey research also tells us that three in ten men believe women's advancement has come at their expense.[36]

Unsurprisingly, opinions about women's progress differ widely along partisan lines. The Pew organization reports that three-quarters of Democrats (76%) say that the country hasn't gone far enough when it comes to giving women equal rights with men, while 19% say it's been about right, and 4% say the country has gone too far. Among Republicans, a third say that the country hasn't made enough progress, while 48% say it's been about right, and 17% say the country has gone too far in giving women equal rights with men.

---

[34] "Women Business Owner Statistics" https://www.nawbo.org/resources/women-business-owner-statistics_[accessed 9/3/22]

[35] "College president statistics by gender" https://www.zippia.com/college-president-jobs/demographics/_[accessed 9/4/22]

[36] "A Century After Women Gained the Right To Vote, Majority of Americans See Work To Do on Gender Equality" https://www.pewresearch.org/social-trends/2020/07/07/a-century-after-women-gained-the-right-to-vote-majority-of-americans-see-work-to-do-on-gender-equality/_[accessed 8/31/22]

The Southern Poverty Law Center has identified many virulently anti-woman organizations,[37] noting that both white supremacy and male supremacy are driven by fear of a perceived loss of white male status. "Politicized arguments about issues such as reproductive healthcare and anti-trans legislation echo far right concerns with maintaining hegemonic white male power and asserting control over marginalized group's bodily autonomy, as well as their social, political and economic agency."

The question we confront is not whether a majority of Americans want to return women to "barefoot and pregnant" status. They do not. However, as we have seen with the assault on abortion and reproductive autonomy, an assault opposed by large majorities of Americans, an ideological minority focused on a single issue can defeat the preferences of a significantly larger number of citizens for whom that issue is one among many. Whether Americans would see that scenario play out in the current backlash to women's autonomy was the question that prompted this book.

Early in the run-up to the 2022 midterms, conventional wisdom predicted a Republican wave, or at least a vote sufficient to give the GOP control of the House and Senate. Then the Supreme Court handed down the decision in *Dobbs*. The immediate effect was summarized in a New York Times essay written by Tom Bonier, a Democratic political strategist and the C.E.O. of TargetSmart, a data and polling firm.[38] Bonier began by acknowledging that, over the last few years, Americans had consistently "acclimated to some very grim realities" and observed that no matter how grim, Americans have seemed unwilling to exact political consequences for those realities. When reactions to the unprecedented leak of the *Dobbs* decision proved to be relatively muted, he assumed that pattern would hold.

Once the actual, official decision came down, however, everything changed, as Bonier notes:

> For many Americans, confronting the loss of abortion rights was different from anticipating it. In my 28 years analyzing elections, I've never seen anything like what's happened in the past two months in American politics: Women are registering to vote in numbers I've never

---

[37] "Male Supremacy" https://www.splcenter.org/fighting-hate/extremist-files/ideology/male-supremacy [accessed 9/1/22]

[38] "Women Are So Fired Up to Vote, I've Never Seen Anything Like It" https://www.nytimes.com/2022/09/03/opinion/women-voters-roe-abortion-midterms.html [accessed 9/4/23]

witnessed. I've run out of superlatives to describe how different this moment is, especially in light of the cycles of tragedy and eventual resignation of recent years. This is a moment to throw old political assumptions out the window and to consider that Democrats could buck historic trends this cycle.

In the wake of the enormous and shocking victory for reproductive rights in Kansas,[39] Bonier analyzed voter registrations in the state since the *Dobbs* decision had been handed down:

> As shocking as the election result was to me, what I found was more striking than any single election statistic I can recall discovering throughout my career. Sixty-nine percent of those new registrants were women. In the six months before *Dobbs*, women outnumbered men by a three-point margin among new voter registrations. After *Dobbs*, that gender gap skyrocketed to 40 points. Women were engaged politically in a way that lacked any known precedent.

> Repeating the Kansas analysis across several other states, a clear pattern emerged. Nowhere were the results as stark as they were there, but no other state was facing the issue with the immediacy of an August vote on a constitutional amendment. What my team and I did find was large surges in women registering to vote relative to men, when comparing the period before June 24 and after.

Bonier's essay was published in early September, and encouraged as he was, he was unwilling to offer a prediction for the November election. As he wrote, all election predictions rely heavily on past experience, and there really was "no precedent for an election centered around the removal of a constitutional right affirmed a half-century before."

For a number of years, the GOP has been a minority party, depending for its electoral successes on gerrymandering, vote suppression, and the activism of pro-life single-issue voters. The lack of a similar level of activism by pro-choice voters was a consequence of the widespread assumption that the courts would protect Roe and their access to reproductive autonomy—an assumption that allowed them to view

---

[39] Ibid.

abortion as just one issue among many. In the wake of *Dobbs* and in the run-up to the 2022 midterm elections, that dynamic seemed to have changed. The question was, had it changed enough to overwhelm electoral history and the conventional wisdom about midterm elections? Would the loss of reproductive autonomy generate enough intensity and turnout to carry the day?

The answer to that question, we are gratified to note, was a qualified "yes."

Chapter Six: When Mama Ain't Happy, Ain't Nobody Happy

Sheila Kennedy

The results of the 2022 midterm elections stunned the pundits and political observers who had anticipated a politics-as-usual rout of the party in control of the White House—especially this time when the omens, if not dire, were definitely very negative. President Biden's approval rating was hovering between 41% and 44%, far lower than the approval ratings of Presidents whose parties had lost control of Congress by large margins during their first midterm elections. Inflation was a huge issue at over 8%. A substantial majority of Americans insisted to pollsters that the country was on the wrong track. All of these indicators and a number of polls signaled the likelihood of massive Democratic losses.

And then those losses failed to materialize. The Democrats held the Senate and lost the House by a margin small enough to complicate, if not crush, Republican plans to thoroughly upend Biden's agenda. To say that these results were unprecedented is an understatement. And while it is never accurate to attribute an outcome to a single cause, the data clearly highlighted the overwhelming importance of women's votes.

The gendered politics that we have come to recognize, and the women's vote that upended 2022 midterm expectations, didn't suddenly emerge from a void. Women have been registering and voting at higher rates than men in every presidential election since 1980, and the Center for American Women and Politics at Rutgers tells us that the so-called "gender gap" has grown slightly larger with each successive presidential election. Women, who constitute more than half the population, have cast almost 10 million more votes than men in recent elections. In the most recent midterms, according to CNN, women constituted 52% of the electorate and men 48%. According to exit polls, 53% of those women voted Democratic. In a swipe at the pundits who'd discounted the probability of a massive women's vote, Hillary Clinton tweeted, "It turns out women enjoy having human rights, and we vote."

The growing political participation of women hasn't been triggered solely by the cultural changes in the status of women that we have been documenting in this book. The ongoing and increasingly visible breakdown of America's political infrastructure and the threat that breakdown poses to America's continued democracy has also motivated women voters, who see that breakdown privileging the hard-right, MAGA Republicans who pose the greatest threat to women's continued progress.

The widespread perception that the Republican Party is anti-woman is a relatively recent phenomenon. When the female co-author of this book ran for Congress in 1980, she won a Republican primary in deep-Red Indiana, despite taking explicit pro-choice and pro-gay-rights positions. Those positions were not uncommon among Republicans at the time. Over the ensuing years, however, as the GOP has become steadily more dominated by Evangelicals, cultural conservatives, and Christian Nationalists, the party has become increasingly hostile to women's rights, at least as most American women define those rights. Female voters have responded with a growing preference for Democratic candidates.

In 2022, the *Dobbs* decision, overruling *Roe v. Wade*, supercharged what was already a substantial gender gap. It brought women who had not previously voted to the polls, energized much of the Democratic base, and caused not-insignificant numbers of Republican women (who had previously felt protected by *Roe v. Wade*) to vote against ballot measures restricting abortion and for pro-choice Democratic candidates.

The Political Context

In 2022, American women cast their ballots in an electoral system that has gotten steadily more distorted, with distortions that have worked to advantage Republicans and disadvantage women. Over the past several decades, Republicans have engineered structural advantages, allowing the GOP to achieve wins in far more races than the party's percentage of the vote would otherwise have delivered. The party has both facilitated and benefited from the steady erosion of the country's democratic practices, participation, and norms. That erosion has been widely described and deplored; it has also been attributed to an equally wide variety of causes, from Republican successes in gerrymandering to educators' emphasis on STEM and the corresponding neglect of civics instruction.

Gerrymandering may be the single most destructive element of that electoral dysfunction. It has clearly undermined democracy and voter choice; in a rapidly urbanizing country, partisan redistricting has given rural voters (who reliably vote Republican) disproportionate political power. Thanks in part to the way in which gerrymandering discourages Democrats in Republican-dominated states from casting ballots and partly to demographic shifts that resulted in thinly populated states having the same two Senators as densely-populated states, the last Republican Senate majority was elected with twenty million fewer votes than the Democratic minority. Gerrymandering allows the GOP to control state legislatures with supermajorities, even when voters prefer Democratic candidates by hundreds of thousands of votes. It has thus nullified elections and insulated lawmakers from democratic accountability. In the run-up to the 2000 election, the nonpartisan Cook Political Report calculated that only one out of twenty Americans lived in a genuinely competitive congressional district.

Of course, it isn't only gerrymandering. The vastly increased use of the once-rarely-employed Senate filibuster makes it incredibly difficult to pass any legislation. In its current iteration, the filibuster requires sixty votes, a legislative supermajority, to accomplish anything. And then, in addition to the effects of anti-democratic gerrymandering and perverse use of the filibuster, there's the Electoral College. No other country has a similar mechanism. The Electoral College was first developed to protect the electoral competitiveness of America's slave states. Today, thanks to population shifts, the Electoral College gives vastly disproportionate weight to rural voters and thinly populated states. All of these mechanisms have allowed a purportedly democratic America to be governed by a shrinking political minority.

Much of the political dysfunction that America is experiencing is due to the failure to adapt our election laws to the social and technological changes the country has experienced over the years. The ubiquity of computers especially, has allowed partisans to throw a lot of sand in the gears of the country's electoral systems. The problems are widespread but may be most acute in the U.S. Senate—a chamber paralyzed by its own internal rules and insulated from the popular will by a 230-year-old formula for unequal representation. The Senate has become a firewall allowing a shrinking minority of mostly white, conservative voters across the country to block policies they don't agree with and safeguard the voter suppression tactics that shore up Republican power.

Democratic senators currently represent some *forty million more* voters than Republican senators, a disproportion hardly reflected in the Senate's nearly even split. But in the absence of any modifications, it's poised to get even worse. According to an analysis by David Birdsell of Baruch College's School of Public and International Affairs, by 2040, 70% of Americans will live in the fifteen largest states and will be represented by only thirty senators, while 30% of Americans will have seventy senators voting on their behalf.

The precarious status of our democratic systems has been the subject of numerous books and articles, and it is not our intention to repeat or belabor the significant scholarship that attempts to explain and address these problems. It is important, however, to recognize that these very real problems not only prevent the country from engaging in genuinely democratic self-government—making a mockery of the ideal of one person, one vote—they also pose an obvious threat to women's continued economic and political progress. That is because, as democratic systems

73

falter, it is the theocrats and rightwing populists who stand ready to assume control. The growth of populism over the past decade has been global; in the United States, its appeal is based largely on nostalgia for an imaginary past in which "those people"—Black, Brown, female, gay—knew their place and no one questioned the rightful dominance of the White Christian male. To say that such a worldview threatens the progress women have made is to belabor the obvious.

So here we are. For the past fifty years, assisted by technologies that decreased household burdens, changes in the job market that made brute strength less important, and buoyed by laws advancing legal equality and Supreme Court decisions securing the right to control their own reproduction, American women have made steady economic and political gains. *Dobbs* leveled a direct attack on those gains, and America's women understood the extent and implications of that attack. As Moira Donegan has written, *Dobbs* didn't simply negate women's right to bodily autonomy, it also threatened women economically:

> It is women whose prospects shape the economy, women who are workers and consumers; it is women who dream to advance economically, to retire or finish school or buy a house; it is women whose economic prospects, along with their health, dignity and freedom, have been curtailed by *Dobbs*.[40]

The question posed by political strategists and media pundits was straightforward: would enough women understand *Dobbs* in that way, and would it matter politically?

The Midterm Election

Dobbs mattered. Democrats did not lose control of a single state legislature that they held prior to the election; a result not achieved by the President's party during a midterm election since 1934. In addition, Democrats *expanded* control of Michigan's House and Senate, Minnesota's Senate, and Pennsylvania's House. Democratic gains at the gubernatorial level were the best since 1986 and notably saw the election of a significant number of women governors, bringing the total of states headed by a female chief executive to twelve. Meanwhile, holding the Senate was a stunning outcome; on average, the party in power loses seven seats in the

---

[40] "We were told abortion wasn't an important election issue. How wrong that was" by Moira Donegan, https://www.theguardian.com/commentisfree/2022/nov/11/abortion-important-election-issue-wrong [accessed 11/24/22]

U.S. Senate. It has gained seats exactly four times since 1934. In the House, the party in power loses, on average, 26 seats. Although Republicans won the majority, it was by a single-digit margin.

As John Hendrickson wrote in The Atlantic on Nov. 4, 2022, "concerns over the future of reproductive rights unequivocally drove Democratic turnout." Hendrickson's observation has been confirmed by several polls. In a *VoteCast* survey[41], pro-choice voters, who took the position that abortion should be legal in all or most cases, were far more likely than pro-life voters, who said that abortion should be illegal in all or most cases, to say that the Supreme Court's decision overturning *Roe v. Wade* had a "major impact" on which candidates they voted for. The gap was more than twenty points: 55 percent of self-described pro-choice voters said *Dobbs* was a major factor in their decisions, compared to 32 percent of self-described pro-life voters. When analyzed by party, the gap exceeded thirty points: 65 percent of Democrats said *Dobbs* was a major factor, compared to 32 percent of Republicans.)

The Bulwark is a relatively new media outlet, founded in 2018 by Sarah Longwell, Charlie Sykes, and Bill Kristol, who had all defected from the Republican party in the wake of Donald Trump's 2016 election. All three continue to consider themselves politically and philosophically conservative, and they brought those conservative *bona fides* to their analysis of the impact of *Dobbs*. The publication ran an analysis on Nov. 11, 2022 by William Saletan titled "The Data Have Spoken: Abortion Was a Decisive Issue in the 2022 Midterms." Among other evidence, Saletan cited both the *VoteCast* poll and an exit poll that had been jointly sponsored by a group of television networks:

> In the network exit poll, 60 percent of the respondents said abortion should be legal in all or most circumstances. Twenty-seven percent of voters said abortion was the most important issue in casting their ballots. Democrats won both of these groups—the 60 percent and the 27 percent—by about three to one. Sixty percent of voters said they were angry or dissatisfied about *Roe* being overturned, and more than 70 percent of this angry-or-dissatisfied majority voted for Democrats.

A Nov. 11, 2022 article by Niall Stanage in *The Hill*, a nonpartisan political news site, echoed that conclusion. It found the issue of abortion access to be "a vital factor in securing a better performance for Democrats

---

[41] "AP VoteCast" https://www.norc.org/Research/Projects/Pages/ap-votecast.aspx [accessed 11/13/22]

than almost anyone expected.... Those who chose abortion as their top issue broke more than 3 to 1 for Democrats. Seventy-six percent of them voted for President Biden's party and 23 percent for Republicans, according to the main national exit poll."

Just over a hundred years have passed since women finally secured the right to vote. The recent midterm elections have made it very clear that most women in America have no intention of relinquishing the hard-won rights that followed their enfranchisement, including the all-important right to control their own reproduction. Thanks to their determination, we don't think it is an exaggeration to suggest that in 2022, the votes of American women saved democracy.

American Women Saved Democracy

While the "chattering classes" were still churning out their reactions to the mysterious non-appearance of a red wave in the midterms, the majority of those analyses echoed that of conservative New York Times columnist Bret Stephens. In his weekly back and forth with liberal Gail Collins on Nov. 14, 2022, Stephens summed up Democrats' surprising performance by concluding that however American voters might feel about inflation or crime or the overall direction of the country, they weren't ready to give up reproductive rights, endorse election denialism, or cast ballots for "Republican candidates who have the intelligence of turnips and the personalities of tapeworms."

As data has continued to emerge in the wake of the midterm elections, the enormous importance of reproductive rights to the election results has become increasingly obvious. All five states with stand-alone abortion measures on the ballot voted for women's bodily autonomy, including deep-red Kentucky. More importantly, in virtually every state, turnout by women—a number of whom had only recently registered to vote—increased.

That increase was consistent with the longer-term trends reported by The Center for American Women and Politics at Rutgers and discussed previously: women have registered and voted at higher rates than men in every presidential election since 1980, and the turnout gap between men and women has grown slightly larger with each successive presidential election. In the 2022 mid-terms, not only did women outvote men, they sent a message that was unmistakable: American women are not going backwards, and they are not handing their reproductive choices over to state legislators.

It's important to note that it isn't just through the emphatic message sent by women voters in the midterm election that women are protecting

America. They are pursuing justice and the rule of law in other forums as well. In Georgia and New York, it is women prosecutors who are conducting important investigations into the illegal and anti-democratic activities of former President Donald Trump. Fulton County District Attorney Fani Willis has been intrepid in her inquiry into Trump's efforts to steal the 2020 election by browbeating election officials into "finding" additional votes in Georgia.

A Brookings Report focused on Willis' dogged pursuit of those engaged in promoting what has come to be called "the Big Lie." The report enumerated the multiple efforts made by Trump and his associates to subvert the election results in Georgia and concluded that those efforts violated several relevant criminal statutes. At this writing, the Georgia grand jury proceedings are ongoing.

Meanwhile, in New York, another female Attorney General, Letitia James, sued the Trump organization for fraud. James won an important interim victory in that office's ongoing lawsuit against Donald Trump and the Trump Organization, when a New York court granted her motion for a preliminary injunction that prevented the organization from conducting business in New York State. The court found that the claims in the lawsuit were likely to succeed at trial. Subsequently, those claims did succeed, and the Trump Organization was found guilty of several counts of fraud.

Going into the midterms, there was considerable debate about whether American democracy would prove robust enough to withstand the obvious and significant challenges it is facing from White Christian Nationalism and what we've come to call Trumpism or MAGA Republicanism. Protecting democracy and democratic governance requires adherence to one of the most important elements of the rule of law: the principle that no one is above the law—not rich people, not celebrities, not elected officials, and not former Presidents.

That essential principle is one of the multiple aspects of American governance that Donald Trump and his corrupt cohorts utterly failed to understand. If there was any one thing Donald Trump clearly believed, it was that rules are for other people; that they don't apply to him. One of the very few Republicans who has had the courage to tell him otherwise when he was still the most powerful figure in the GOP was yet another female: Congresswoman Liz Cheney of Wyoming.

Thanks to America's women, the United States dodged a bullet in 2022. The significant number of people who want to take the country back to an idealized and fictionalized past lost, and while proponents of gender equality, both male and female, didn't win in any permanent sense, they lived to fight another day.

What that "other day" will look like is the subject of the Afterword.

Afterword

In this partial history of the women's movement, we have explored some of the technological and social changes that narrowed the once-wide gap between male privilege and female subservience. We know that this exploration has left many important questions unanswered. Furthermore, what we cannot know is what happens next. Where do we go from here? Is women's progress coming at the expense of men's well-being, as some pundits are warning? Will we eventually reach a place where gender is but one element among the many attributes of a given person, or will the "battle of the sexes" continue? If that battle continues, what form will it take?

Among the many concerns that we have not been able to study adequately are these:

1. How should proponents of women's rights respond to accusations that the movement thus far has disproportionately emphasized—and benefitted—white, privileged American women? Are there efforts underway to extend the benefits of greater equality to women of color, here and abroad? What is the movement doing to identify and ease the barriers faced by less educated, less affluent women? In other words, is the glass ceiling only a concern of those who are already poised to break through it?

2. It is clear that, at this stage in its evolution, what we call "the women's movement" has developed significant internal fault lines. (Perhaps it always had those fractures; as Marcus likes to point out, Gloria Steinem and Bella Abzug appealed to rather different constituencies). Are there new leaders who are recognized across those fault lines? How do their goals and the goals of the various factions diverge?

3. What will be the longer-term effect of *Dobbs*? This is an issue about which the co-authors differ. Marcus believes that *Dobbs* was followed by a retreat rather than an advance. He acknowledges that women did come out to vote in greater-than-usual numbers in 2022, but he characterizes the gains as victories in skirmishes at the expense of the larger battle, a splintering of the movement. Rather than focusing on a single national objective, he believes that progressive women have allowed the reactionary Right to

shift attention to a variety of other conflicts: transgender issues, efforts to ban library books, and the general war over "woke-ism." This rerouting has dissipated the energy that would otherwise be focused on women's reproductive and economic rights. Kennedy disagrees, believing that *Dobbs* and the Right's continuing efforts to control women's reproduction have acted as a wakeup call to the significant percentage of American women who were previously non-political or complacent, believing themselves to be secure in the right to control of their bodies. Those women recognize the centrality of reproductive freedom to women's equality and the threat to their liberties posed by *Dobbs*, and they can be counted on to focus the majority of their efforts on regaining control of their bodies. Once awakened to the importance of political activism and the mounting dangers of rightwing autocracy, women have predictably extended their activism to matters beyond abortion and birth control, correctly seeing those assaults as elements of an overall illiberal, statist, and dangerous philosophy. Only time will tell which of the co-authors has read the situation correctly, but both emphatically agree that **the fundamental right of persons to determine the course of their lives and the well-being of their families** is the central issue of our time—and that it is an issue that doesn't just affect women. It strikes at the heart of the American conception of human rights.

We began this book as an exercise in social history. The *Dobbs* decision was handed down a couple of months after we began researching the path that women had taken—a voyage we've dubbed "from property to partnership"—and it underscored the importance of our goal for this effort. *Dobbs* was a frontal assault on human liberty. The decision was widely seen as a "shot over the bow" of women's right to self-determination, but in reality it was much more. It was the expression of a growing, profoundly anti-liberty worldview that poses an existential danger to fundamental American constitutional values.

What *Dobbs* didn't change was our underlying goal for this little book. In order to look forward and to act with vigor, we need to understand the technologies and cultural changes that have empowered women over the past years.

Now, people of good will must enlist the technological and cultural opportunities of our times to issue a call to arms. This effort, this manifesto, if you will, is intended to assist in a marshaling of building blocks for the critically necessary program to stem the tide of reaction, to regain what we have already lost, and to prevent the further erosion of women's personal autonomy. It is the time for all of us to ask, "What else are we at risk of losing?"

In the Introduction, we quoted from a Dylan song—an anthem for a turbulent time. We conclude with another verse from a challenging decade, this one from Peter, Paul and Mary:

Don't let the light go out,
It's lasted for so many years
Don't let the light go out,
Let it shine through our hopes and our tears.

About the Authors

Sheila Suess Kennedy is Emerita Professor of Law and Public Policy at the School of Public and Environmental Affairs at Indiana University Indianapolis, and a former Executive Director of Indiana's ACLU. She blogs daily about policy, culture, and politics at www.sheilakennedy.net.

Morton J. Marcus is an economist and former director of the Indiana Business Research Center at the Kelley School of Business, Indiana University. He co-hosts a popular podcast, *Who Gets What?,* and writes a long-running newspaper column on economic issues concerning Indiana and the nation.

www.ingramcontent.com/pod-product-compliance
Lightning Source LLC
Chambersburg PA
CBHW070503220526
45467CB00002B/553